T0146562

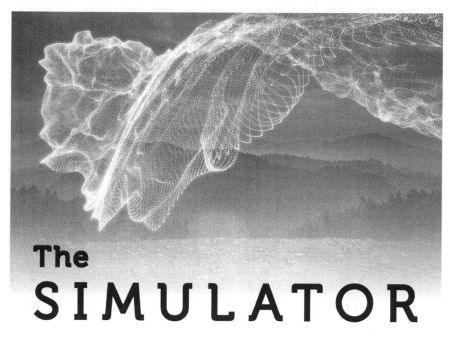

The
SIMULATOR

a dream within a Dream

FRANK SCOTT AND NISA MONTIE

BALBOA.
PRESS
A DIVISION OF HAY HOUSE

Copyright © 2015 Frank Scott and Nisa Montie.

All rights reserved. No part of this book may be used or reproduced by any means, graphic, electronic, or mechanical, including photocopying, recording, taping or by any information storage retrieval system without the written permission of the author except in the case of brief quotations embodied in critical articles and reviews.

Balboa Press books may be ordered through booksellers or by contacting:

Balboa Press
A Division of Hay House
1663 Liberty Drive
Bloomington, IN 47403
www.balboapress.com
1 (877) 407-4847

Because of the dynamic nature of the Internet, any web addresses or links contained in this book may have changed since publication and may no longer be valid. The views expressed in this work are solely those of the author and do not necessarily reflect the views of the publisher, and the publisher hereby disclaims any responsibility for them.

The author of this book does not dispense medical advice or prescribe the use of any technique as a form of treatment for physical, emotional, or medical problems without the advice of a physician, either directly or indirectly. The intent of the author is only to offer information of a general nature to help you in your quest for emotional and spiritual well-being. In the event you use any of the information in this book for yourself, which is your constitutional right, the author and the publisher assume no responsibility for your actions.

Any people depicted in stock imagery provided by Thinkstock are models, and such images are being used for illustrative purposes only.
Certain stock imagery © Thinkstock.

Print information available on the last page.

ISBN: 978-1-5043-4435-7 (sc)
ISBN: 978-1-5043-4847-8 (hc)
ISBN: 978-1-5043-4436-4 (e)

Library of Congress Control Number: 2015918377

Balboa Press rev. date: 1/7/2016

Contents

Preface

It is impossible to detect the **Simulator**, unless you are able to get out of its box that contains you....

Difficult to perceive, it hides in subtlety, a layering that is superposed in such a manner that one's senses catch only that which becomes uploaded to the brain and converted into a mind-world construct—the reality we experience from moment to moment. It is impossible to understand, for the instrument itself, the mind, is found within its precinct.

How do we escape the Simulator?

We must find *the well* within.

The Well

Within each of us the placeless place

Flows with Radiance Full—

Filling the room of uni-verses.

Sun-warming, it serves

To light hearts

As they alight

Like butterflies anywhere in the Garden

Of His Heart,

The emanations of Mystery

A secret Spring

Feeding the well until, beyond

thinking, it overflows

With His desires of Love to bestow,

If only we would drink.

*

Detection of the *Simulator*, the main program running everything, the Dream outside the entity's dream, occurs as an act that delineates each level of its layered, embedded, and superposed components through the Soul-based state of awareness, accomplished through the Creator's inscrutable and mysterious Will and Pleasure. More specifically, in order for the entity known as human to qualify or graduate from one to the next level of awareness, the entity in the role of a male or female must surrender further within his or her heart to the All-Knowing.

This letting go of one's egoic desires is easier said than done. The ego's programing nature, a group of sub-routines that grow in number the older one becomes, sometimes masquerades under the pride of being morally or ethically *right*, or even of having the knowledge or the understanding of God's Word through the latest Manifestation or Prophet. Only the Omniscient One can see within each heart the true purpose and intentions seated therein.

Thus, as has been said by many Wise Ones, *the only true Judge is God*.

Moreover, when created, the *First Entity* (the Manifestation of God) went through a process of acquisition, of Self first from the creative process of God within, followed by the actions that brought about the engraving of His Image, and the gradual Revelation of His Beauty. The Entity thus acquires and acknowledges its *I-ness* and *Being-ness,* and is heard to state,

"I am aware!"

God's first act in the process of revealing His Beauty is witnessed in the creation of a **Perfect Being**—a Manifestation of His own Self.

This Perfect Being, a Manifestation of God, integrates as the First Mind, and is able to express the words,

"I am aware that I am aware."

Once having emerged in physical form, the Perfect Being, and First Mind, is able to say,

"I am aware that I am aware that I am the Manifestation of God."

Without the Perfect Being's ever-present existence, throughout creation, there would not be a Creation. The Perfect Being is the Voice within all His creatures. For as long as the Voice within is listened to, entities exist as expressions of a potential in transit and transcendence within the *Simulator*, and are given opportunities to graduate from that mind-world construct within the unified system of intelligent life. When the Voice of God is ignored, the entities find themselves pursuing their own fancies, egoic or selfish modulations (self-programming), and moving further from the Truth that will set them free from the worlds of names and appearances, of Un-reality.

These worlds of creation beg for recognition and attention, yet fail to show us the Truth of our journeys. What remains is a loop that repeats itself, another opportunity once again to hear the Voice within. Each entity must hear His call to Surrender, Remember, and Return, acknowledging that there is only one God, Who does what He Wills and Pleases.

This life, one of many temporal and fractional, existential experiences, only has value as far as its contribution to the Divine Plan. All material substance being illusory—spiritually speaking— the value of each thought-form, feeling, and action is determined by the unified system of intelligent life in terms of whether it creates, for the individual entity, a direction of approaching God and further serving His desires, or moving one further from the Creator by serving selfish inclinations that result in an unsatisfied state of being corrupted and/or perverted.

One can determine the direction of one's spiritual course in a simple manner—through the emanations received by one's spiritual heart. Should God's Love be flowing through that portal in response to the entity's being in service to Him, the individual will feel predominantly joy. Should the heart's portal be blocked or interfered with as a result of incorrect moral choices of the individual, the predominant feeling experienced will be sorrow.

The moral gradations appearing between total service and total disobedience will produce the range of feelings, from bliss to anger to death-like depression.

Sometimes, that which the individual entity experiences may be caused by events not linearly-linked, time-wise, to the present life. These events may be understood to have occurred as a result of actions taken either by that individual in past temporal and fractional, existential experiences in other worlds, or by relatives of that individual who created actions of spiritual relevance (either positive or negative) to that entity in present time. These events may result in a spiritual benefit by creating the opportunity for greater nearness to God, or in a detriment that must be reconciled or atoned for in order to allow one to continue advancing upon the straight path to God.

The best and surest measure, to assist all of us in our sojourns of growth, is that of surrender to the

Will of the Living God, the Creator of All. By doing so, we may experience His world of Creation as He designed it—bereft of any and all interference from His creatures' desires derived from their limited understanding.

Surrender of the creature in all aspects—from Soul to Spirit to mind to body—yields the best outcome for uniting with the Beloved of all the worlds. According to His Will, God may even, through His grace and mercy, lift His servants out of the realms of births and deaths to the heavens of endless life, lit by *the Eternal Sun of His Love*.

Chapter 1 - Questions and Answers

What is of interest and worthy of our attention is found in the relationship between our states of Knowingness, and the quality and type of questions we propose to ourselves. Our states of Knowingness are derived from our many temporal and fractional, existential experiences. Each of these chapters of our narratives written on the Scroll of Existence has a value, in terms of whether it brings us closer to, or further from, the Truth. This Truth is none other than the understanding of the nature and purpose of Reality!

Experiences fed by egoic desires foster and continue to nurture Un-reality, the traps and loops that keep the entity, known as human, imprisoned in Un-Knowingness. People may be caught by their roles as a man or a woman, following various scripts, using whatever props, practicing this or that belief system, under this or that other tradition with its particular rituals, speaking a certain language, living in this or that region of the planet, in this or that country, state, and community, whether single or married, with or without children, with varied educations, and influenced by a diverse culture, or not. All of these third- and fourth-dimensional factors create layers of loops enmeshing the entity in its own circular logic and direction, a condition that fosters certain questions and brings about answers that perpetuate a third- and fourth-dimensional state of consciousness for the most part, sprinkled with an occasional dive into the fifth dimension, or higher. Inspiration, deriving as it does from the

Universal Mind (the fifth or Spirit) or higher levels, is thus truncated, and the advancement of humanity becomes imperceptible, at best.

The type of questions that help a human entity transcend must propel and bring about the unknown as part of one's awareness, beyond the third- and fourth-dimensional, sense-perceived material condition, and mind-world construct. The human entity must arrive at that moment when the question or questions can no longer be answered locally. That is, the questions and resulting answers *must address the Eternal and the All-ness that reside within*.

This moment is referred to as *enlightenment,* the true purpose of the journey of growth, remembrance, and return. When a human entity begins to address aspects of his or her existential experiences, the whys of life beyond the third- and fourth-dimensional parameters of its temporal and fractional properties, he moves towards Paradise—as a state of being.

When a human entity arrives at that stage of inner development, this quality of questions surfaces into his or her physiologically-based state of consciousness, inviting the entity to address the essence of who each of us is, beyond the mind and body, and even further than the Spirit that manifests all creation.

The *Simulator* will respond to the quality and type of questions posed, and will bring the relevant answers regardless of whether these bring us closer to, or further from, the Truth. The unified system of intelligent life brings about the answers, with all the necessary special effects, to leave no doubt of the nature and relevance of these questions and answers in one's journey.

Death brings to bear no influence on, or finality to, the continuation of one's journey. Reward or punishment, happiness or sorrow, represent road signs that assist us to navigate temporal and fractional, existential experiences. *Knowing* or not are simply conditions that indicate the need to obtain more information, and to come up with the right questions. Individually or collectively, the quality of our lives together—our relationships, interactions, and exchanges—are simply signs on the road towards a mutual objective that speaks of our states of Knowingness and Love—how close or far we are from that ultimate experience of humanity's true destiny as given by God.

The quality of the lives of each individual entity is determined by the level of Spiritual growth, how each of us is influenced by, and manifests, from that imperceptible field of activities (the fifth dimension, the Spirit), along with the intentions and attitudes affecting that which we carry out and execute upon. More spiritual growth equals to a happier, more fulfilling life that continues to change according to our further growth towards our intended objective— service to one's Creator, as the basis of perfection.

This concept of service many be understood in various ways; as Jesus said,

"What you do to the least of my creatures you do to Me." Service to one's family, neighbors, and community has its place. Nonetheless, it is not a substitute for being consciously aware of one's total surrender to the Lord of All names and attributes.

With this understanding, and acting upon it, each member of the human family may move forward towards the world of light and eternal life. God-willing, humanity as a whole will be raised to the level of a functioning, harmonious unit acting on behalf of—and carrying out—the divine Will and Pleasure.

In addition, the level of Spiritual maturity, the individual range and scope of influences based on our innate capacity—one's Knowingness—varies.

Some are destined to move quickly and some slowly. Whether quickly or slowly, steadfastly or waveringly, all people will eventually find their way to a life of perfection ruled by the King of all the worlds—the All-Knowing, All-compassionate, Lord of All. Praised be God.

From the point of view of the *Simulator*, the choices we make, when coming upon each emerging situation in life, are reflected in the appropriate outcome, with the results meant to serve our states of Knowing and Loving. The opportunities will be there always to reflect and to learn. It is up to us. If we choose not to learn from our experiences, the events will be recorded below the threshold of our consciousness, whether we are able to remember them or not, affecting future outcomes in a positive or negative way that brings us closer to, or takes us further from, our ultimate goal—a state of Self-fulfillment, with a sense of the continuing purpose of service both to the Creator, first and foremost, and to our kind, as we gradually advance as a unit towards establishing a divine civilization.

For those whose understanding or state of Knowingness has yet to become consciously aware of a Creator, the question about the existence of a Creator becomes appropriate. This is perhaps the ultimate question. What happens when an entity asks him-Self or her-Self that question, and waits for the answer? The question itself reflects the present state of Knowing of the individual. An unwillingness to ask and/or wait for the answer indicates a certain level or grade of spiritual development; not asking that question also indicates the level or degree of the heart's spiritual growth. Within the *sea of conscious-awareness*, to be given that question by the Simulator is to have an opportunity for further enlightenment, challenging each one to measure the degree of his or her connection to the whole of life, or alternatively, the disconnection resulting from an egoic, limited understanding.

When the entity reaches the stage of development that invites that question, the Simulator will provide the necessary experiences leading to the asking, and the answering. As we move nearer to, or further from, the Divine Plan, collectively and/or individually, society and/or the individual will be moved towards having the necessary experiences that assist in bringing that realization collectively or individually in response to the overall maturity of society, or the spiritual development of individuals.

Everything is in synchronicity and in tandem around the globe, reflecting the many complex interactions that result in both groups and the individual being directed towards, or away from, the intended goal of a divine civilization, beyond the survival of the species, third-dimensionally speaking.

This complex integration by stages distinguishes society's quality of spiritual life, both as a whole and individually, and forms part of a design within the Divine Plan. The result is a gradual advance as a unified field of activities that arise from their *imperceptible* origins as a reflection of the many intentions that are found hidden within each human entity's heart, and the more *observable* effects carried through each and every action executed in the theater of life, whether as part of one specific domain and species, or external and far-off activities, beyond our planet.

Much of the activities that take place third-dimensionally remain unobservable, because they are too fast or too slow, too small or too far, to be sense-perceived, and therefore be a part of our fourth-dimensional, mind-world construct as a segment of our understanding.

This inability to perceive globally most of the flow of activities, ever-present and surrounding each of us, results in the impression of a disconnection and separateness from, and non-inclusion with, the whole. This illusion of separation is further strengthened by the diverse individual interests which attract us. Each of us is left unaware of the entirety that would have contributed to a more complete point of view and the understanding required to properly function here on Earth.

To make up for this natural inadequacy and its effects, a higher dimensional state of conscious awareness can be accessed to bring the appropriate understanding assisting our decisions at any given moment, provided we are connected and paying attention, with the right intentions, for everyone and everything participating in the experience of life. The Simulator is there to supply every needed condition with all the necessary special effects: an array of sensory and emotional, psychological and instinctive, physiological and spiritual conditions, to best serve each sentient being's overall learning curve. We are thus immersed in a creative process affecting everything and everyone, living and non-living, from the mineral to the human, here on this planet, and everywhere else for that matter, within a Divine Plan carried out through a unified system of intelligence that ultimately gives and brings Oneness.

Chapter 2 - Love and Loops

You are here on Earth, in part, to demonstrate the efficacy of an eternal companionship. What is the use of a love between two immortal light beings if it is only for a moment within the scheme of eternity?

The purpose of an eternal companionship is to foster the growth of each individually, and, of course, both together as a team, towards the One True God. Without this lofty and entirely necessary goal, the two will wander off like two ships in the night—unable to find each other for many lifetimes, upon the deaths of their mortal frames.

In a broader sense, our purposes are measured by the quality of our experiences, how we manage them, and how our choices, attitudes, and intentions bring about their fruits. What are we trying to be? What are we trying to know? To possess? To go to? All these questions may be only partially realized, as the domain within us invites us to return and continue our journeys of exploration and discovery. These subconscious loops keep us focused in and on the fractional and temporal, existential experiences as we transit and transcend from one to the next world, searching for answers without formulating the right and complete questions—as we each stand alone *as proof of our own Reality*.

Each of us in our own journey shares a frame of reference in a theater of interaction and exchange. Each one of us shares more than just a third-dimensional world construct. Each one of us integrates within our Selves and with each other through mind and Spirit, yet we feel and think of our-Selves as separate, distant, and disconnected from the whole wrapping us all into one unit that has yet to behave like one, and become its true-Self.

We are lost within a quagmire of illusions, our own vain imaginings, as the *Simulator* responds to every whim and desire from its members; it is designed to sustain the illusion of an ever-changing reality that brings about all appropriate outcomes in response to the inner conditions of each individual's heart and mind.

Time and space within the Simulator bring about a relative set of effects according to the properties determined by local physics, thus enhancing the experience of everyone. While immersed in the **Sea of Awareness**, in wave form, each entity may emerge consciously in particle form—having a material body, gravitationally formed and structured, internally functional, carbon-based, and electromagnetically operated, until the **switch** is turned off, and the entity leaves the body behind to move on in Spirit (the wave condition) conditionally, as a sphere of pure awareness.

Endless experiences demonstrate to the potential light Being that the desire to *become god*, a desire born from the erroneous assumption that we each are in total control of, and rule, our destinies (rather than allowing God to lead us without resisting) is actually *the greatest trap* ever designed and placed into practice.

This trap, or ever-present loop, runs through omni-dimensional systems of unified intelligent life, with multi-directional outcomes possible as the reflections of an infinite, inner reality of the deluded entity who knows no bounds, is unguided by the Creator and His Manifestations, and is therefore unable to connect beyond and outside his own limited knowledge. Circumscribed by his own lack of capacity to Know and Love as a result of the pursuit of selfish desires, the entity fails to Remember and Return to the Beloved of all the worlds—unless he chooses to surrender his own will and desires to those of the One that created him. By answering to the **Clarion Call** of the Manifestation of God for the day and age of his or her emergence into a local state of consciousness from the **sea of awareness**, the Soul-possessing light Being may be freed from the never-ending loops of mortal lives, and catapulted into Paradise.

Such is the Divine Plan, built with myriad possibilities simulating a reality observed and experienced by every participant, yet leaving room for those experiences that are unique to some, and those significant to one individual alone. This seamless operation embraces the entity in such a way that it leaves little doubt as to its impact upon each being's mind-world construct. Even birth and death are special effects of the Simulator, which subtly moves the entity from one to another world, in order to advance each entity's dream within the Dream!

To understand this Dream of the Great Spirit, one must have the certitude that all the universes and the creatures contained within them are simply reflections of the Love of their Creator. That is to say, the quality of life of each sentient being is dependent upon that entity's ability to receive, and be thankful for, the Mystery of God's ineffable Love.

This Love is presented to us in three forms: That which is modulated from on High (upon the individual as a carrier wave), that which is transmitted between the creatures in the form of compassion and empathetic understanding, and that which is realized from within, oftentimes as a result of a crisis within the individual's life in which he or she loses everything, and is thereby greatly encouraged to surrender completely to the Omniscient Presence.

As it has been said, the Creator enlightens the heart of whomsoever He chooses. When the individual entity is overwhelmed by God's Love, there is nothing else.

This indefinable state of being submersed within God's Love can be described only by its resultant effects upon the individual's behavior. One becomes caring of others and of one-Self—having no purpose save the carrying out of God's Will and Pleasure, realizing one's Self as less important than the sub-atomic particle, and understanding God as the Great Spirit, the Life-Giver of All.

This blissful state or condition is that which sustains life at all levels, within and outside of the Simulator, in balance with, and trusting in, the All-Knowing One. There is nothing else!

In order for all the inhabitants of Earth to live together in harmony and peace, it is necessary for our Love for, and obedience to, our Creator to be of paramount importance in all interactions of a personal, or public, nature.

Without this Love, life loses its magical luster derived from following His Will and Pleasure. With this Love, all events move forward as smoothly and easily as a river flowing across a bed of sand.

This Love is the purpose for living. When the creature and the Creator are linked within the shadow of God's Great Love, nothing can harm the poor, helpless creature of dust. When the creature is unaware of this Love as the basis of life—and all lives—he or she wanders through endless stretches of time, bereft of a compass to navigate the waters of illusory, temporal existences.

In the *central portion* of the Soul lies the key to the destiny of each individual. The Soul is like a honeycomb made of layers within layers. Each layer contains the next layer, much like the *skins* of the onion. Within the innermost layer is the true **God** *"particle."* This is actually neither a *layer* nor a *particle*, but a portal through which God, through His Manifestation, speaks to each of us in His still, silent Voice. This portal, tenth-dimensionally speaking, is like the old-fashioned telephone access between the Creator's heart and each of our hearts, with the *switcher* who connects us being the **Manifestation of God** for the place and time in which the creature exists.

What is relevant here is that the *communication line* must be clear of all interference with that Love, for any imbalance, caused by such qualities as anger, fear, jealousy, and greed, will interfere with the divine signal.

When the heart receives the clear signal of God's Love, then the Soul's portal rings with the confidence that derives from the connected entity's Knowingness that he or she is Known and Loved by God, and therefore the entity gratefully not only responds to that Love, but also bathes in, and surrenders all personal desires to, serving that Love. With infinite gratitude the sentient being is consciously aware of that Love being the basis of each event, at all times.

The Soul, Spirit, mind, and body meld in service to the All-ness and All-Mighty-ness of the Creator, and in this state or condition we each are blessed with the Knowledge that,

I am no more than a speck of dust, and I am the true, beholden, servant of God, here in existence to serve His Will and Pleasure for as long as He desires, which is to say, forever. This is the meaning of Eternal Life.

In the timelessness of eternity, God's Love lives on. It has neither beginning nor end, range nor scope. It simply is, without rhyme or reason.

It exists of Itself, by Itself. It cannot be distinguished from Its Creator Who Knew of this Love within. It is Itself creative and continually Self-creating.

The Love of God encompasses All. Like the wind that circles the Earth, there is no point where it is not.

We thank God for His Love, for without that Love, we would cease to exist—would never have existed. As the apple is a product of the tree, and cannot be conceived of without that parent tree, we, tiny creatures in the immensity of the time-space continuum, cannot be conceived of without our Creator's over-spreading and protective branches.

We spring from *that, and to that* we return—in the endlessness of the One Day of Paradise.

This is the Palace of eternity, where neither time nor space exists as a condition, and the purpose of life becomes clear: to wed one's heart to the Eternal One.

There is no other desire of the entity.

This all-encompassing Love which reaches into the heart of each Being cannot be measured. It is the All-in-All, the purpose of every experience of each sentient being—no matter how insignificant. In fact, it is this Love of the All-Compassionate One that is the *clay* from which He molds every living being. Of this we can be sure, and for this we can be grateful.

It is this ineffable Love that allows the functioning of the universes of all the worlds—both seen and unseen.

It is this Love which allows the human lovers to love each other, the animals to procreate, even the plants to grow towards the sun.

This Love is the reason for every Word, and for the endless scrolls of existence determining and recording the lives of an infinite number of entities.

It is the Sea without Shores, the wind beyond skies.

It is that which motivates all to live in harmony and peace, even joy. Thank God for His Love.

Tonight, as in almost every night, the planet Earth glows in the light of the moon. The moon reflects the light of the sun, then shines upon the Earth. In this manner the people of the Earth have light from the sky at night.

Analogously, when the people can no longer perceive the Sun of God's Love and Truth themselves, the moon of the Manifestations of God is sent to reflect God's Will and Pleasure, and to illumine for a humanity in darkness the path to God.

In this way, the people can find a lit path to nearness to the All-Knowing One. Their ignorance is washed away by the light of the full moon: the Words of the Manifestation illuminating their hearts.

Chapter 3 - The Flow

There are two conditional flows or systems through which packets of information are transported along scalar waves, running through the Simulator. The first, and most important one, is seated as the foundation to the entity's eternal existence, *the Soul*, bringing about a tenth-dimensional state of awareness: the ***I am aware that I am aware***, a state bringing about the fundamental condition of immortality to bear its fruit directly upon the creature.

God ***Knows of His Love***—an eternal engine that creates and sustains—for each entity, as an act that engraves His Image from within His creature, now forever aware of His Revealing Beauty. The Eternal

Divine Life created by this Love has neither known beginning, nor known end, and fuels the state of a Being of Light attainable through that Portal, a Soul-based state of awareness which can be called **Knowingness**.

The second conditional flow or system that Reveals His Love, is *the Spirit,* seated fifth-dimensionally. As the engine bringing about all things, the Spirit binds eternally a Creation with purpose and meaning unto Himself, and animates everything everywhere, the created and/or manifested, with **His Love**.

The first, Soul-based state or condition can be addressed as the Hidden and the Un-manifested. The second, Spirit state, as fields of imperceptible activities, is the precursor to that which is manifested, *and can be observed third-dimensionally*, no matter how small or large, near or far, or slow or fast *that material reality is*. The Spirit is the life of Creation.

The Spirit of creation (these imperceptible fields of activities), imposes by stages the necessary integration of all its parts into a cohesive Whole that represents the universal mind as a unified intelligent system. The universal mind acts upon the **vacuum**, a plenum, third-dimensionally, as the source of all that becomes manifested as part of the fractional and temporal existential experiences within each plane, and track of existence.

The universal mind connects everything into a conditional unity realizing the oneness that defines His Creation, a colossal, unified system of intelligent life, animate and inanimate, composed of mineral, plant, animal, and human life as expressions of their respective Spirits. The latter entities act as observers and participants, learning to interact with everything and everyone. Gradually, they come to higher states of conscious awareness and remembrance until they gain access and return to their divine station, the zenith of Being-ness, as fruits of His Divine Plan.

During the return to the *pure state of awareness* as, the entity gradually progresses in its heart's state of purity, two conditional flows animate the entity eternally—***Knowingness and Love***. The flows of Knowingness and Love are, however, circumscribed by a process that requires all entities to elevate their attentions, focus their love, and purify their intents, as they approach Him in order to experience the fulfillment of His Divine Plan for each one of His creatures.

The gradual acquisition by God's creatures of the **Knowingness and the Love** of God's Plan, executed through His Manifestations, those Luminaries that bring Salvation, *is the way out of the Simulator.* Thus, entities must show forth their ever-present states of knowingness and love by recognizing God's Manifestations as the Revealers of the Divine Plan, and the Educators of all entities. By gaining access to Their Message—the Revealed Word—and implementing those directives in their lives, human beings may achieve a closer state of being illumined, remembering and returning, redefining their directions, and fulfilling each of their missions to bring about the true advancement of an eternal civilization.

Recognition of these Divine Messengers is followed by the entities' acceptance and obedience to the Lesser Covenant (as delineated in the Ten Commandments), those innate dictums that guide their relationships with each other and with everything, enabling *the necessary unity* in the body of mankind as an initial step, and the unity of all creation as the final objective.

Acceptance of, and obedience to, the Greater Covenant follows, where every entity in creation acknowledges and is bound by that recognition that *signals the Oneness* of it All, through His Manifestations of Power and Might, of Love and Mercy, of Forgiveness and Illumination, understanding that They are All One and the Same.

As a consequence of this timeless understanding, the Soul-based awareness within, announcing such a realization of imminent enlightenment, the entity's love is offered. From within one's Soul, the ever-present flow of Divine Love becomes a *conscious* existential experience that invites and brings about the completion of one's search for the Beloved, thus beginning the attainment to one's divinely, pre-ordained station as a servant of All-Mighty God.

*

Entities are piped through shuttles of light within the Simulator, gated out or in, and subject to modulation, the integration by stages of information that translates into that which is experienced. There are three sources of information; the first originates from the Soul, deep within the core of who we are; the second source emerges upon the arrival of the entity in a world to be experienced—the environmental factors such as genes and other local circumstances that begin their influence; lastly, egoic-based choices form experiences to be undertaken to mold the character of the entity throughout this fractional and temporal, existential experience.

All entities experience life through time, energies, mind, and body; these factors provide a physiologically-based state of consciousness. If fully integrated, the entity's experiences, during each third- and fourth-dimensional sojourn, contribute to an overall Soul-based state of awareness producing enlightenment within—as a Light Being. This condition of enlightenment is seen as a *light hue* representing a grade in development.

One of the authors can testify to this fact from a personal experience in which he died briefly, and was brought back to life after having visited the other side as a sphere of pure awareness.

The more clear and evanescent the *hue of light* adorning the being's *state of pure awareness*, the further (towards higher, more perfect realms) that entity's next shuttle exit will be. The less clear the hue of light adorning the entity's state of Soul-based pure awareness, the shorter the trip between worlds (the less the being advances spiritually). The entity thus is either progressing (moving into more advanced worlds), or regressing (moving into less advanced worlds) along this pathway of growth, moving incrementally throughout the Worlds of God.

There are many cases where the entity's light hue is absent and remains indistinguishable from the vast darkness of empty space that surrounds the entity's presence. When this is the case, that entity is unable to enter the *light shuttle* that would allow the transfer to other worlds of God. The entity remains in a loop that traps and engulfs that Being in less-developed systems of intelligent life, where opportunities are given again for further spiritual development, in a new role, script, and the necessary conditions relevant to the state of being.

The creature is either advancing towards the intended objective of his Creator, or is regressing farther and farther away, into the world of dark primitiveness that surrounds each incoming, fractional and temporal, existential experience.

Creation, the Dream of a Creator intent on the completion of an Eternal Plan, is re-created each time the Tree of Life is renewed. This Blossoming is symbolic of the timely and positive effect that occurs when a *Manifestation of God* dispenses *Divine Information* upon planets like our Earth.

These planets serve as way stations for the development of entities who are potentials in transit and transcendence, moving from one to another world, as each entity grows in Knowingness and Love.

When Those Who dispense Divine Information root Themselves upon the Earth, from within the fifth-dimensional state (the mind of the universe and the home of the Spirit), the Words or Information flowing through each Manifestation of God, time-specific, begin to reach, and seed, the soil of the hearts of men.

The light emanating from these leaves of the Tree of Life, like hands, exhibit in the land God's Vision for humanity, bringing those that respond to the *Clarion Call* and the shades of His Mercy, which purify and bring the necessary advancement. These acts of Mercy and Grace of the Beloved bestow upon humanity a New Life, by breaking the loops of each one's journey so that remembrance and return may begin.

The fullness of this Tree of Life, symbolized by Its many green leaves and robust presence, indicates the tower of strength each Revelation represents to the world of mankind, to those in waiting, the many creatures that will join the ranks of the faithful.

The sturdiness and strength of Its roots, that break the subfloor of the human heart filled with vain imaginings and passions, enable the roots of Knowingness to sink into the rich soil of the Earth's faithful beings. Responding to the influence of the Presence guiding them on the straight path towards God, the faithful rejoice as the Tree's roots shear through every obstacle as the Tree grows, attracting others towards the Palace of the Beloved.

The descent of this *New World of the Soul's* longing overlays upon the present world of dust. The result is that faithful pairs of companions, who carry out the command of the All-Knowing, leave comfort and security behind to follow the orders of the Divine Master now modulating their lives.

The revival of lives to be obtained, experienced, and expanded throughout the world, obtained from this higher-dimensional point of entry, can be witnessed in those entities who respond to the Divine Master; though the numbers may be small, these blessed Beings of Light live the life of Divine Guidance, sprinkled with the rain of His Mercy and Grace, and lit by the *Sun* of His latest Divine Revelation.

Seek then He Who offers Eternal Life. Find in Him the Word that sets all beings free from the adornments that have imprisoned and locked them in loops, moving them further away from the Truth of their journeys.

Chapter 4 - Viewpoints, Paths and the Mirrors

Since time Immemorial, communities have arisen with different values, even opposite viewpoints, adding contrast to the way we have lived. On the one side, stand those groups whose behavior ostensibly favors cooperation and teamwork. However, since they do not have true unity based upon deeper spiritual values, and are, instead, rife with egoically modulated and driven, competitive agendas, under the guise of individual *"freedom of choice,"* their groups' cohesiveness dissolve under the weight of unsustainable stresses.

The members struggle under the burdens of debt and overwork, family breakdowns and crime, addictions and mental disorders, and many more problems.

On the other hand, there are those communities that do not hide their rapacious desires for control and power, which status they obtain, temporarily, through competition for supremacy and survival, regardless of the means used to obtain these ends. Sheer force and enslavement, dictatorial actions, sudden bursts of brutality and the resultant fear-based control, allow the few whose arrogance knows no bounds to enforce submissiveness upon their populations.

We think of these types of communities as resulting from *"natural"* forces, or instinctive activities. We assume humanity will always act without a common direction, without considering the well-being of all. We accept, and have all come to expect, that once in a while these contradictory ways must clash, and bring about change at whatever the price. Like the beasts of the field, there are those, most, that become the prey, and those others, fewer in number, that behave like predators.

The purpose of civilization is to advance the cause of humankind in the direction of the One True God. Anything that impedes that progress to the detriment of the Soul's nearness to God is not of *civilization*, but of *dis-integration*.

Those who pretend to be working for the advancement of humanity through, for example, scientific or industrial developments whose true purpose is to be used as destructive forces upon life, do a disservice not only to the body of mankind as a whole, but also to themselves, individually. The use of technology designed for life's destruction reverses the direction of humanity's development—from ascending upon the path towards God to descending on a road leading to the hell engendered by greed, envy, power, control, and other destructive and selfish passions as expressions of ill-conceived notions from distorted minds and perverted hearts—*a state of Unknowingness*.

Once heading down the latter road, filled with the darkness of shame and regret, human beings have only the Great Light of the Manifestation and Emissary of God, sent by His Grace, to illuminate and sooth the suffering caused by the entities themselves. This infinite illumination offers the remedy to all, restores the well-being of humanity, and lights the path back to the Kingdom of Love—and all good virtues—that has always been awaiting the Soul-possessing Spirit Beings, creatures of humanity at the end of the rainbow of obedience and complete service to the One Lord and Master of Creation.

Without the Light of service within each servant's heart, life upon Earth (or any of His worlds) has no purpose, and the way is barred to nearness to God, obscured within the fog of selfish passions and vain desires.

Let this missive be a lesson and reminder to you who waver with weak will from *the straight path* towards He who created you as His creature and humble recipient of His overpowering, all-Encompassing Mystery of Love.

Should you be at a moral cross-roads in your life, choosing between a life well-loved and well-lived, with God as the cornerstone and the foundation and reason for the bowing edifice of thy Soul, or a house built upon the material and physical pleasures of the moment (such as sexual passion), may you choose wisely in a way that will advance your love and understanding of that sacred mission given to you as a gift before you were born, and that awaits your acquiescence to its divine precepts in accordance to the eternal Will and Pleasure of He who rules all with justice and compassion.

The views we hold, and the paths we choose, must be understood in relation to where we stand as reflecting mirrors. Are we reflecting God's Dream for us, or our own dream/nightmare created from our limited understanding?

Third- and fourth-dimensional perception consists of a *mirror-like Effect* that offers and gives clues in terms of what we see, how we interpret and view this world, and why most of us are not conscious of other worlds around and beyond us.

Our first impression tells us that what we observe is symmetrically reversed: just as what we observe in the mirror image's left side corresponds to our right side, and equally, the mirror image's right side is but a reflection of our left. Is there any significance there?

What can we learn from a mirror's properties as we embark on an understanding of omni-dimensional states of conscious-awareness, and multi-directional venues that lead somewhere else?

When the mirror of the Heart is cleared of all vain imaginings and earthly desires, a sudden reversal, third-dimensionally speaking, takes place, and the beauty and perfections of a higher domain are superposed, replacing any previous anomaly; it simply disappears—the Vision of true Reality unfolds, reversing what is with what it should be!

We can think of our True Selves living in the Eternal Realm in God's perfect world—in a state of potential transit, until our Creator deems we are ready to be realized and to join His Domain.

Our focus of attention from Pure Awareness is projected through a point into the fifth- and then, into a third- and fourth dimensional world within the Simulator that is the Reflection of the mirror of the Heart and Soul. The more purified one's Heart and Soul, the more the reflection creates a world of more perfections for us to participate in.

When our Hearts and Soul reflect the purity of God's Will and Pleasure for each of us, then we no longer need to descend with our attention to mortal worlds as tests of our Faith; like Alice who went through the Looking-Glass, to the world behind the mirror, we can return from that backwards world to the *living room* of nearness to God—completing our True Selves as servants of God and lovers of the Beloved.

We exist within the Creator's Dream, the Great Simulator. Within that Dream, all entities carry on their own dreams within the Dream—their simulators, or mirrors, that reflect the myriad possible outcomes derived from each heart.

All possible outcomes are built-in within the Great Simulator, pre-ordained recordings as tracks that become the life we appear to live and experience. Changes brought about by the personal choices of any one entity can move that entity to another pre-existing track, accommodating the choice made, and carrying out the effects of that choice within a set of circumscribed commonalities that give the appearance of a reality lived and experienced with others whose choices develop into interactions and exchanges, as a basis for a global theater and a civilization which may or may not achieve continuity as part of that mutually adhered-to track in time.

This complex arrangement of all probable outcomes requires thus an omni-dimensional, unified system of intelligent life, able to absorb and maintain such an immense and complex scenario in one and all the worlds of God. There is no escape from within this creative process, guiding every one everywhere towards one common end. In the midst of what appears, at times, to be a chaotic system and in disarray, there is one force guiding the All towards that Oneness and Unity that reflects the only Reality, His Dream, however our personal realities may seem to contradict that divine indivisibility.

Entities are continually jumping from one to another track within the Dream to accommodate their different grades of Knowingness, moving forward as each one progresses, or backwards in response to a regressive pattern resulting from individual choices.

These jumps are so fast that the entity is unable to consciously determine that a shift has occurred, and even death within our track of time may provide a jump into another track to continue the experience of living as an alternate outcome, as if that former choice and event never took place.

Each track of time and space offers to the traveler in eternity the opportunities to grow in Knowingness and Love. Each life track is perfectly connected to the flow of experiences preceding it, and will continue connected to the one or many that follow seamlessly.

The memories available in and during the entity's sojourn in one specific track are quite relevant and always make sense. The entity thinks and feels, remembers that life experienced and lived—except when one or more events have damaged the unit (the body) used during that sojourn. In that case, there are other tracks, as alternate outcomes, that will at some point be embarked upon to continue the journey of Self-development.

Regardless of appearances, and they are numberless, the life you live with all the experiences you remember, is what it is, and you are trapped and exist within it—the loop and narrative written in the scroll of your existence—the recording and its multiple-track system.

You are conscious only of the one life you are meant to be focused upon while in that track of space-time. For as long as the conscious switch is on, you will come and go every day, sleeping, dreaming, and awakening, almost as if this life is all there is. The dreaming state hints at your true existence as being part of an omni-dimensional, multi-directional, and non-linear system. If the conscious switch goes off, you will come to another track in the space-time continuum of your narrative written on the scroll of existence, one that continues with additional fractional and temporal, existential experiences, each and all a part of His Divine Plan for you as His creature, guiding you (reeling you) back towards Him.

The Love of God functions like a magnet, regardless of the present state of Knowingness of the entity. The entity was created as a potential in transit and transcendence from one to another world of God, the Lord of all the worlds. ***Remembrance and Return*** are a function of the Divine Plan of the Creator. The entity must find the One that Manifests God *for the day and time* of that entity's immersion in the Sea of Awareness—while emerging on the shores of consciousness, incarnated in a body, and reflecting the ***Mirror of the Soul***.

Reward and punishment can be observed and perceived as shortening, or prolonging, the over-all journey of Remembrance and Return. The quality, or lack of, in each of the immersions and emergences from the Sea of Awareness onto the Shores of Consciousness may be seen as instrumental in offering opportunities for the exploration leading to the discovery of He Whom God made Manifest.

It is thus incumbent upon you to pray to God that, during your present sojourn, you are brought to such an experience, to be awakened or resurrected, integrated from within (Soul, Spirit, mind and body), and guided to fulfill your mission in life and, as part of your existence, be brought to the company of your eternal companion.

Those who have the thought that creation is purposeless and without a direction, with little significance other than for those fit to continue within one mortal existence, do not bring joy either to themselves, or to others. Competing and scheming to control what is necessary to bring a better life for themselves, they reduce the burden of their third-dimensional construct at whatever cost; saddling nations with liabilities both financial, ethical, and moral for the many, they serve the interests of the few; planning for the short run, their only consideration is that which is necessary to succeed and remain ahead of others; these entities, empty of Soul and Spirit, bring great harm to all of life. Instead of encouraging Unity with God and within humanity, their actions engender temporary alliances in the name of expediency, where disloyalty and specious changeability become acceptable, even expected: today you are my friend, tomorrow my enemy.

Politics serving the few becomes the norm of a society bereft of the right direction and guided by skewed information manipulated at all levels, including that of the press originally established to inform the populace of the relevant news of the day.

Such is the plight of a society in disorder, disdaining the Plan of God, and ignorant of a Reality that will eventually emerge as the supreme standard, sweeping away the old illusions born of the egoism that stands in the way of true progress.

Be conscious of God's patience; as has been revealed in many Holy Scriptures over time, His Wrath will replace His Mercy to deal with the mischief-makers.

Chapter 5 - Unity and Oneness

The conditional unity throughout the Simulator, the Dream that encapsulates everything everywhere, is based on natural and moral laws or principles, addressing the third- and the fourth-dimensional constructs.

Natural law ensures an order of things everywhere, and becomes for the entities a challenge to be discovered and explored, and eventually learned and understood, to advance their fractional and temporal, existential experiences through proper use and management, reducing their burdens and/ or enhancing their stay.

Moral law or principles, that guide all entities towards a unity- based systematic approach to all interactions and exchanges, rely on the Lesser Covenant (such as the Ten Commandments). This agreement all entities within creation understand as essential to the management of all processes that blossom from mutually beneficial activities, resulting in the advancement and sustainability of a civilization being formed by, and carrying the collective interests of, all inhabitants.

We understand that this agreement underlies all our interactions. It is fundamental to all aspects of our relationships, between us, and with everything around us. The Prophet and Divine Manifestation Moses wrote down the main aspects of this covenant.

The Ten Commandments, as they are known, were made a part of the entities' journeys of separation and return. Innately pre-ordained and recorded within each and all tracks delineating each and all possible outcomes, based on each one's decision to adhere to, or ignore and violate, *the Laws from God*, these guiding principles are embedded within the main program running the Simulator, the Divine Dream. They affect all our dreams within that Dream.

As inescapable as it sounds, an innate guidance is available to all entities as a compass. When the Soul-possessing, Spirit Beings of Light follow God's Laws, the Lesser Covenant, their inner compasses point towards the **Pole Star** of Paradise. The Laws of God guide each and all spiritual travelers through the sojourn of immersion in the Sea of Awareness, to emergence upon the shores of consciousness. They then each acquire a body to partake of each and all necessary fractional and temporal, existential experiences. Thereby, all entities eventually *Remember their True Purpose, Return from their journeys of separation,* acknowledge and surrender to the Lord of all the Worlds, and experience at last their reunion with their Beloved, an act that completes their realization and acknowledgment of the reason for being created: to experience at last the Dreamer's Dream.

This climax, outside of time and space as we know it, in a beginning that knows a start in each of us as Beings of Light, subjected to enlightenment, and filled with the Love of God, knows no end.

This Reunion becomes a banner illumining all the entities' actions along the journey of Remembrance and Return. The obedience to the Divine Will is required for the safe and swift completion of each sojourn, so that, with the least difficulty and suffering, all may acquire the intended attributes adorning their station as creatures of God.

The prolongation of suffering, associated with each choice fueled by selfish desire and vain imaginings within the Simulator, is meant to discourage thoughts and actions not in alignment with God's Will and Pleasure, His Dream for us, and thus to assist in each entity's sojourns. In the midst of a darkness surrounding the entity's disconnection from the right path of exploration and discovery, the Divine Law guides and serves as a light. When the traveler chooses that which enhances life, the positive response from the Simulator engenders a feeling of inner joy as a sign that creature and Creator are being reunited.

It is a way to guide the entities within them-Selves, as they maintain the connection to the Immemorial Root, and each one integrates by stages the Soul-based state of awareness with the Spirit (the imperceptible field of activities), mind, and body. This unity is then expressed in the third-dimensional material construct, and within the mind-world assembly, including thought-forms hormonally-charged with emotional content. When the body (or unit), used during the earthly sojourn, is connected to the Spirit and Soul, the creature becomes a true servant, able to explore and discover through the relationship with his or her Creator, and with everyone, and everything, how to collaborate and bring about a better world for us all.

To obtain this condition of unity within and without, we must come to the One Who is the Source of this integration, Who reinvigorates and fulfills all entities' eternal journeys of remembrance and return, including that spiritual union experienced through the pairing phenomenon—an eternal companionship—throughout all the worlds of God.

Such an integration, enriched by the wisdom from the latest Manifestation of God, along with the loving certitude arising from an eternal companionship, allows each seeker to find fulfillment and wonderment in unity.

This collective unity—based on the agreement of the Lesser Covenant, ruling all of our interactions and exchanges throughout the journeys of exploration and discovery, in each and all fractional and temporal, existential experiences, exists to assist within the Simulator. This unifying integration of Soul-based awareness is a light on the Shore of Consciousness. The compass within, the Soul-based awareness brings these two points of Reference, the spiritual with the material, into an alignment that serves to guarantee the absence of any distortion or skewed viewpoint, as we assemble a fourth-dimensional state of conscious-awareness during each of our journeys of separation and return. We must remember that this separation had a purpose, to explore and discover, from within, each of our individual gifts adorning our uniqueness as entities created by God, our Lord, and, the ultimate Goal of our exploration and discovery.

It is evident and clear that the content of the Lesser Covenant, the Commandments ruling all interactions and exchanges among entities, and between each entity and all aspects of creation, carries a moral significance and influence related to the results of the entities' actions. If they have disregarded and violated these Principles, they will find themselves in loops that take them further from *Knowing their True Selves*. Obeying God's Law, on the other hand, brings nearness to one's eternal Self, and the Creator of one's existence.

The Simulator's purpose is to bring about a reality that reflects all actions taken by one and all of the members of its unified system of intelligent life, locally and universally tallied. Everything and everyone is tied together into a single process and unit that admits no separation, and brings about the realization of the significance of the saying that this *one world is our planet and our home*. Leaving no doubt or ambiguity, the result of the Simulator's program reaffirms the fact that there is only one creation and one Lord. He created one unified system of intelligent life, affirmed by the regular appearance of His Manifestations, Who in turn are One and the Same—a Oneness throughout Creation confirming the Greater Covenant assuring the Order of it All.

Throughout Creation, there exists a constancy confirming the existence of God. This constancy is brought about through the actions of the Simulator. From planets to galaxies to universes, throughout all the myriad varieties of life, all sentient and intelligent beings are brought to acknowledge their participation within the Divine Plan carried out through the Simulator.

They are all inside a purposeful Simulator. In this way the Creator, the Great Spirit, the Unknowable Mystery, Ever-Transcendent, guides the development of all of His creatures endowed with a Soul-based state of awareness. In this way, He helps each and all remember and be able thus to return as created and designed, with all the adornments of a divinity that highlights such a station and Reality.

The Greater Covenant of Oneness is exhibited in the Manifestations of God. Transcending our limited understanding, They were created as Universal Educators. Linked throughout the worlds of creation and revelation with the Power and Authority of God, the Creator, They oversee as One Person and the same Divinity. The affairs of all entities, in their individual and collective journeys of separation, remembrance, and return, are under the jurisdiction of the Messengers of God, leaving no doubt as to Their common purpose. Their history, throughout infinite eons, brings about a narrative that binds and bonds all sentient and intelligent creatures to the understanding of the ultimate purpose, significance, and direction of each of their individual journeys.

Through Their steadfast lives and Their Words of Truth, They demonstrate how to follow the Straight Path, and avoid loops that engender separation— how to remember and return to one-Self, while serving others.

This narrative is repeated, time and again, by the Manifestations representing the Creator of All. The dispensing of Divine Information revealed by Them is time-specific, and is given by Them, as Educators of humankind, according to the capacity and need of the collective. Given the existing distortions resulting from entities' current divisiveness, distortions of the Spirit which further the descent of all entities into the abysm of perdition, each Manifestation of God has a monumental task for His pre-ordained, divinely-appointed, time-period.

To extend, and continue using and practicing, any one of these Dispensations beyond Its appointed time brings about a perversion of the Text (misinterpretation of the Word), when the interpreter is modulated solely by environmental and egoic desire. The programs resulting from this perversion of the Truth fit the needs of *those now living outside the time continuum for which It was originally designed.* Such a perversion results in the further corruption of the behavior, the weakening of the morals, and the multiplication of the points of view among those entities using information from an earlier Dispensation. Consequently, the social order is further fragmented into a myriad of belief systems (dogmas), now centered on the incorrect understanding of the *Divine Purpose.*

As a result, over time, the heart of each entity is negatively affected, and the Spirit of Life in the heart becomes absent, bringing about the emergent need to address one's intentions, and to restore him-Self or her-Self to the good graces of God. Without His blessings, life is hard—even brutal. With His blessings, life has a chance of being tolerable. Even with the pain and suffering that are inherent in the life of an Earthling, the blessings of God give hope that the human (by agreement) being will be lifted by Him to a higher plane of existence.

In order to receive God's blessings, it is necessary to follow the rules given by His Manifestation for the day and age of each creature's emergent state of consciousness. There are the reasons for the rules established by each of the Messengers of God, from such ones as Abraham and Moses (the Ten Commandments), to Jesus, Mohammed, and those most recent. These *rules* are only useful as a guide to the true seeker who already has given heart and soul to the Lord. Otherwise, they are impossible for the ordinary human to fulfill.

When each Messenger of God comes to deliver His Message, He comes with a specific time-frame (as previously stated) in mind for which that Message—the Word of God—is useful to the advancement of humanity. Before that time, humanity will not have the capacity to understand the Message. After that time, every one thousand years, more or less, according to conditions and Divine decree, the Message will not have the power

Cling to honesty, sincerity, purity, integrity, and the like, and do not let the thoughts of earthly possessions disturb the sanctity of the human heart.

This fleeting life is only for the purpose of purification, for weeding away those who turn their backs on their Creator, from those who cling to Him for their very lives.

There is nothing else but God's Pleasure.

There is nothing less that the insignificant **pleasures of ego-driven desires** that ultimately translate into injustice towards all.

Choose well, fellow traveler. Choose well. Let nothing dissuade you from the ultimate achievement of this life, the goal of all fractional and temporal, existential experiences: unity with God's inscrutable Will and Pleasure.

Without that unity, life has no purpose. With that unity, life continues eternally with an ever-deepening and enriching Purpose. Choose well.

Without justice and unity, the Oneness from within, and from without, remains hidden and unseen.

Chapter 6 - The Handlers

There is an eternal mandate that flows from the Origin of All, applicable to all sentient intelligent entities throughout: *service* to one another. How is this service performed and delivered in an omni-dimensional and multi-directional unified system of intelligent life, beyond third- and fourth-dimensional constructs, in an ever-developing and ever-transcending Realm?

Those that oversee our growth here on Earth, from outside of the Simulator, are entities of a higher development than we are. Their work is to lead those who are willing to listen to *higher realms of understanding* and *greater depths of Love*. This is done through the process of a Soul-based modulation, the integration by stages of signals, or information, fifth-dimensionally of the Spirit, upon each being as a stand-alone, scalar carrier wave.

The entity who is receptive will send out a *signal* along the wave system. This *signal* is received as a sign that one is ready to advance in Spiritual growth. Those of a higher development who are assigned to that entity then transmit the information required to allow that being to ascend a step, or degree, on the *ladder* of spiritual development.

This information may be transmitted through various means: through dreams, visions, books (the Word of God in holy scriptures, for example), events, and words received through subtle hearing, or seeing with the inner eye. The purpose of these transmissions is to bring the recipient closer to God.

Each individual is at a certain unique level of development, and it is the work of the *handlers*, known in some cultures as Guardian Angels, to bring that individual to a higher level of Knowingness when he or she is ready—much as a good teacher brings the ready student to greater levels of understanding.

We are never alone in our journeys. Assistance is always available fifth-dimensionally (Spiritually). We only need to ask.

Higher, more developed Beings of Light can see those in lower levels, although the opposite is not often the case. We are all servants of others, up and down a unified system of intelligent life, interacting directly if sharing the same local plane of existence, or indirectly when communicating fifth-dimensionally and multi-directionally, without the constraints and restrictions of individual capacity, languages, or planetary locations limiting us.

Culturally here on Earth, we have given names to these events when any group or individual from these higher realms makes contact with entities living here on the physical planet. These connections are established with both individuals and groups living on the planet.

These type of contacts do not refer to the ones associated with entities still in the Simulator, although incarnated outside of Earth, perhaps within, or beyond, our galaxy. We refer to entities who have moved, dimensionally-speaking, to other planes of existence—those who were chosen to leave *the oven*, the ones who have graduated.

From the fifth-dimensional viewpoint, we are all communicating all the time, everywhere. Much of this communication is not clear, like the shadowy area around a tree, where the sun's rays cannot be clearly perceived, or an environment so filled with background noise and frequencies that someone attempting to listen to a radio is unable to receive reception. The few signals that are clearly transmitted tend to be received by the untrained, or inexperienced, entity. For unfortunately, those that seek this type of inter-dimensional communication are, for the most part, mainly interested in things of this temporal world—the benefit is thus earmarked for one's fractional and temporal, existential experience.

When the world was young, humanity was just testing its wings of independence. The values of humanity had not yet been established. The descent away from the heights of glory and nearness brought about the separation that fed each being's individuality, a journey of spiritual growth and return. Like a young bird fluttering out of the nest, it might land where it wanted to, or it might not. Either way was acceptable.

Now humanity has been in existence for a very long time; its wings are stronger. The expectations from On High for its achievements are much higher.

Its wings can now take humanity further; it has more control of the direction of its flight.

At this time, humanity is expected to fly towards its Creator. It is expected that its members work in tandem and harmony with each other, and know the rules for doing so. At this time in its evolution, humanity should understand that it will not be allowed to destroy itself over and over.

It is time for humanity to **grow up** and **act its age**. In other words, it is time for humanity to leave the confines of its collective playpen and begin to walk the road of its collective destiny, its pre-destined journey where each one exhibits greater and greater degrees of the divine attributes on the right road to establishing a divine civilization upon the planet.

It is for this purpose, once again, that each of us has been born, and it is for this purpose that the entities known as human continue to exist upon the Earth. God-willing, this purpose will be fulfilled soon.

The *handlers* appear in a variety of ways, whether when announcing something of importance and of future influence, through visions or dreams, or through messages heard, or written, of Truth and prophesies. Materializing enough to be experienced, or remaining invisible, they make their presence known, even intervening to change the course of an event, for an individual, or for a group. These Light Beings may communicate through an ongoing interaction that lasts for some time, enable group visions, or simply assist as God's servants in events like an unexplainable healing, an unexpected solution being given when there was no hope, the serendipitous aid of a stranger, an unexpected accident preventing something worse from taking place, or time being slowed-down, or speeded-up to save people's lives. Near-death and out-of-body experiences, bi-location, guidance, and much more, are more offerings from Light Beings some call Angels.

Every one of their actions has, in the end, one objective—to let all of God's creatures know that they are not in control, that they do not possess anything, and that each creature is absolutely nothing, an infinitesimal point of light in the Infinity of God's All-ness. The handlers thus assist all entities to realize their true and highest stations.

In this state of Knowingness, the traveler ma come to the profound realization of his Soul-based awareness as being reduced to the smallest and most insignificant *dot of light*, allowing only his *Self-awareness of existing to remain*. It is at this moment, alone in the immensity of the infinite darkness of a space holding omni-dimensional and multi-directional unified systems of intelligent life, now unbeknown and hidden, reduced to a mystery unto him-Self, that the traveler discovers that God, too, is His mystery.

The traveler, guided by the handlers, understands that there is a door of Divine Mystery, barring him forever from knowing him-Self, and knowing God. From within this mystery, there emerges a sense of *certainty*, the like of which he has never before experienced.

The traveler has reached a hallmark in his journey of exploration and discovery, and has acknowledged his complete dependency on God—that He shall be His Lord and Master, always. Breaking down in tears of remorse and sorrow, he reconciles the eternity of his journey of separation from within, desiring only to return and experience his Beloved.

The handlers have succeeded, the Simulator has performed as expected, and all is well. The dreamer has awakened finally from his god-like desires, and has removed all vestiges of egotism.

Chapter 7 - Breaking the False Impression

Delusion or aberration mark for the most part a traveler's sojourn of fractional and temporal, existential experiences. Arising from deep within, and for so long, the traveler's vain imaginings and misconstrued perceptions of a Reality long-vanished prevent him from distinguishing what is Real from what is an illusion. He finds him-Self lost within a figment of his imagination. This false impression the traveler believes to be his identity, who he is, as he tries once again to gain the necessary confidence to control, conquer, and amass as much as possible in his quest of wanting to possess that which he can neither keep, nor become. Denying the nothingness adorning his true foundation, he fights once more the fact of his impoverishment, brandishing powers he never had, nor will he ever possess, in denial of any dependency on anyone, fearful of everything, attempting to succeed in a game he will once more lose!

That is the plight of every lost traveler upon emerging on the shores of consciousness from deep within the Sea of Awareness. Totally forgetful of Self, the purpose of his journey, what is important to explore and discover, without orientation, he tries to find a direction, any point of reference that can be used to build a sense of identity, a feeling of belongingness.

He does this as he has done numberless times before, reaching for security from a sense he cannot put his finger on, in an instinctive urge to prolong his survival at whatever cost.

There is an emptiness he wants to satisfy, as he starts once again to pursue an illusory fulfillment. He is impatient, frustrated by the waiting, and by the machinations of his mind and heart. This sojourn may offer something, anything at all, perhaps an inheritance in gold or genes, or even what appear to be opportunities to control others. That which is brought into being is a delusion, though he does not know it. He now lives in the world of names and appearances.

Thousands of years pass, mounting into millions of years, yet they fail to unfold to the traveler something of ultimate worth or importance.

He returns time and again, oblivious of the game he has created, feeds, and sustains, no matter what the role is (perhaps as a male or female, this time around), or the script pre-ordained and pre-recorded to be lived as a fractional and temporal, existential experience, with props, rituals, and traditions, within a variety of cultures and languages, in more- or less-developed scenarios, geographically located here or there, as a potential in transit, in transcendent motion from one to another world.

He has become a seeker of the only Truth that exists in the whole of Creation, yet he is unconscious of it. The Truth gnaws at him, and surfaces once in a while. Without much contemplation, he dismisses the urge to investigate, for another thousand years.

The *Clarion call* sounds again, a reminder heard by many who are called to respond, and to form communities that grow in numbers as time passes, under one name or another, with beliefs that offer reassurance and continuity to those that have identified themselves with its tenants.

To those that do not respond each time around, there are other calls, the ones of the sciences or the arts, perhaps a trade or a business pursuit, or maybe a restful episode of inactivity this time around, on a street corner or under a bridge, the one called having given up wanting the goods most desire, and some possess abundantly. Other entities spend lives seduced by the desire for the intangible wealth of mortal worlds—fame, control of others, or leadership. Others prefer to be followers, perhaps bonded to some ideal, a thought-form structured in a certain way, somewhat different this time around.

To escape these loops, one must ask the right question.... What is the Truth sought after? Can it set me free? Where can I find it? Where do I have to go? Is it near, or far?

We ask these and other questions, more than once, and in more lives than we care to, or can, remember. Life is never the same; games change, and new players participate. Over time, events begin to repeat themselves, here or there, once in a great while. For the most part, we cannot remember, yet on those rare moments, we experience deja vu.

The false impression remains embedded deep within ourselves. What we think of as reality, the illusion and aberration, has trapped us in a labyrinth of tunnels that pipe each of us from one to another world, gated in and out, integrated in stages, and carrying information that feeds us along the way—a loop.

Is there an end in sight?

Suddenly, the monotonous clamoring around the world is silenced. Foretold up to a thousand years earlier, or more, a new Dispensation of Divine Energies is released, so that the process of renewal and remembrance can begin once more. For those that respond, the process of integration with Soul and Spirit begins, the illusion that was falsely impressed upon the inner worlds starts to break, and the veils that separated the lover and the Loved one are gradually removed—the dead are resurrected, and the sleepy awakened.

These cycles of purification are needed to remove the debris and toxins from humanity's Spirit, mind, and body as a unified system of intelligence and life. Over time, the accrued effects of the collective desires and vain imaginings bring about the distortions rendering all entities dysfunctional and disconnected, endangering life on the planet. The Divine Physician returns to heal and educate the world, and prevent the re-occurring drama of self-destruction.

Little by little, the human race is brought back to health, a state of well-being from which to continue its collective development. Righteous choices and positive effects increase, advancing a divine civilization. The activities of all sustain, and allow for, the continuing progress of this planetary, unified system of intelligence and life.

It is not difficult to observe and understand that the body politic of mankind is in need of an Overseer during its sojourn of exploration, discovery, and development. Divinely guided, we can receive, and act from, the wisdom that is derived from these fractional and temporal, existential experiences. It is so easy to lose our way when we are trapped in the third- and fourth-dimensional states of mind and body, without the benefit rendered from the outside intervention that continually assist us as we drive the vehicle of civilization—a map or GPS system given by each Messenger to assure our safe arrival to our pre-destined objective.

It is not only logical, it is necessary to accept, as well as to understand, the need for such an engineering and doctoring of a reality we share over a short period of time, individually, and over a longer period, collectively. We know that there are limitations to our understanding at all times, and that our ever-unfolding narrative, pre-ordained and pre-recorded, purposeful and significant, is taking us all somewhere else, transcending an ever-present moment, through cycles of life and death. We know we are in urgent need to comprehend the Divine Plan of our Creator, who's Love and Knowledge is meant to be experienced by us all. We are not in control, though we think we are. We cannot keep what we obtain, though we think we can possess the material rewards of a lifetime. We think we are in control of the vehicle of civilization, yet we crash, time and again, as a reminder that we are far from the efficient and knowledgeable drivers we think we are. Our technical know-how, a recent event in the course of a recycled time-track, stands as a witness of another attempt of our collective vain imaginings and warped desires to once again *"give it a go"* at controlling a destiny whose destination, we may add, is not understood, either individually, or collectively.

To think otherwise, which we do, is at the core of the false impression of having control and possession of both our destiny and the narrative recording of our baby steps.

Chapter 8 - Coming to ….

The accrual of those moments that help us break through the womb that contains us, only to emerge into another one, a process repeating itself again and again, gives each of us our state of Knowingness. Each moment of enlightenment gets us closer to the death of the old life and the birth of the new one. The cycle, as a process of growth in Knowingness, is not the result of a specific number of enlightenments. No one can tell in advance when exactly she or he will transcend from one to the next moment until it happens; even then, we may be slow to recognize the transition, or even to remember what life was like before the change and transfer from one condition to the next.

At other times, such a change is accompanied by an orbital transfer in understanding, and the traveler can tell, clearly, that he is no longer the same, nor are the conditions and circumstances of his sojourn presenting experiences familiar enough to be easily recognized. Instead, he is astonished during each new encounter.

It is the waywardness of entities, human by agreement, Soul-possessing by design, Spirit beings, piped and gated in and out, modulated potentials in transit and transcendence, that has led to the present catastrophe upon the planet earth. Not much time is left before the planet must be shifted to a new Reality for its very survival. This process cannot be done without the full cooperation of a sufficient number of its members with the divine plan for an unending civilization, a society based on harmony, peace, and the devotion to the Creator's Will and Pleasure.

The catalyst for this momentous change is the human heart. A sufficient number of human beings must cooperate with the tenets of the Greater and Lesser Covenants to allow the phase transition to a higher order of understanding and greater cooperation among all planes of existence to occur.

God-willing—this change will occur soon—before the destruction of the planet, as we know it, is inevitable.

Each node, in a network of unified systems of intelligence and life, itself a component of endless networks that cross and interact throughout an omni-dimensional and multi-directional construct that knows neither beginning, nor end, is of vital importance to the flow of information. This flow translates into what is observed and experienced, as everything and everyone interacts, and the exchanges of information create the means for a comprehensive system of unity and oneness. This system itself is but a node of ever-larger and/or smaller networks, within a Simulator meant to provide a myriad experiences in response to all acts and motions, interlaced and correlating into a whole that remains hidden and far removed from this moment of life.

Despite the immensity of the Simulator, each emergence of an entity on the shores of consciousness is an opportunity to realize the Truth of it all, the certainty arising from knowing one's state of utter *nothingness and genuine insufficiency*, inviting always each traveler, from anywhere in Creation, to come to, and experience, Paradise.

The interesting thing about life is that it is an experiment—God's. We, entities known by agreement as human, are here to experience that which God—through His unified system of intelligent life—wishes us to experience.

No matter how much we think, erroneously, that we are in charge, we are not. The only choice we have is the moral choice between right and wrong. Everything else results from either pre-ordained effects from our decisions, or pre-ordained experiences to *"choose"* from and adhere to in the course of our lifetime. With that understanding, what we are doing with our lives? Are we eagerly looking for the One who can give us the rules for us to distinguish between correct and incorrect moral choices? Or are we wasting our time, in life after temporal life, carrying out a program whose whole purpose is to wake us up to the realization that the only worthwhile thought, feeling, or action is the one to which the Creator, through His **handlers**, has guided us, in order that we may follow the only True Path—the path to His Love.

Without that Love, life is as life-less as a garden of artificial flowers. With that Love, the tiniest action, carried out in accordance with His Will and Pleasure, blooms with an eternal brightness and redolent scent which can neither be described, nor experienced, from a third/fourth-dimensional point of view.

It is the Grace of God that allows the *magic* of life to shine forth upon this, and similar, planets and worlds.

It is the Grace and Mercy of God that allows His Love to permeate every aspect of the lives of His undeserving creatures.

Thanks Be to God for His Love and Mercy for His creatures, allowing their very existence to continue eternally.

*

Beyond the knowledge of all Beings of Light, is the wisdom of the Great Spirit—the Knowledge of the heart. The heart's first Knowingness is of compassion—for fellow travelers and for all life everywhere.

The heart's second Knowingness is of God's compassion—Its infinite and all-encompassing nature.

The heart's third Knowingness is of surrender— the ultimate surrender of all desire as the heart empties itself totally to make room for God's Love.

The heart's fourth Knowingness is of ultimate servitude—the acting from that Love of God under all circumstances, without doubt, with absolute certitude.

When these four aspects of the loving heart are fulfilled, *Enlightenment* can occur—and not before. We come to the realization that there is more to life than what we are experiencing. We begin to ask the right questions, the ones that lead us out of the present bubble of understanding—the Simulator responds with the right answers.

Chapter 9 - Experiences

Everything we learn about our-Selves and others must be experienced. Experiences bring a fourth-dimensional thought-form into action through an act of volition; the resultant output becomes what we Know. Not everything should be experienced, and our choices determine the type and quality of our existential experiences.

Whether these activities present themselves just for the individual entity, a group, or everyone, the result is the same: we either progress in our understanding and ability to do, so that our attention is projected into worlds of greater light, or regress, so that we experience, and be conscious, of worlds of greater darkness.

When those moments appear that become eye-openers into higher dimensional states of awareness, beyond the usual experiences related to daily activities, we can choose to pay attention, or not. These moments can bring us a little closer to the wisdom we all seek—that ultimate understanding about us, about our purpose, and about the reality we all experience.

We can ignore this most important understanding all of our lives, busying ourselves with other things, some seemingly very important, others that remain trivial, at best. Life does come to an end, slowly to some, too quickly and suddenly for others, who may have no chance at all to have the experience of that first step into *Knowingness*.

For those that experience life from one end to the other, over an adequate period of time, they realize during their waning years that there is a diminishing return from a life that is no longer as bright; soon enough, the switch will be turned off. Even with great care, no matter how we prolong that inevitable moment, the body's physiologically-based consciousness ends.

Life is the cumulative effect of our experiences, and our memories of them. A poor memory, or no memory at all, spells disaster at the physical level. In terms of the eternal Self, it is of utmost importance to remember to include one's understanding of the continuum of life, each time we engage in a fractional and temporal, existential experience— early enough, while it still counts.

If, during your life, you have enriched your *Knowingness* of the conditions that exist beyond third- and fourth-dimensional constructs, leading to fifth-dimensional, and higher, states of awareness, you are very fortunate. Knowingness, and the ever-present Love of God, will guide your transit from one life to another as part of your travels, the journey you embarked on long ago. You will look forward to your next life, and be prepared. Having developed and explored your Self during your Earthly sojourn, you will have discovered what was valuable, and partaken of those activities allowing you to experience a Reality of which you will soon be a part.

Because the Creator has built in the Simulator His Desire for us all, we have the option and opportunity to enjoy each and all of those enriching experiences. If we do, we will gradually understand His Will and Pleasure —what those experiences mean, and where they take each of us. We get to know what we need to know, so that we have the opportunities to make the right decisions every time.

We are being engineered into something divine that is not the result of third- and fourth-dimensional experiential constructs, however important these constructs may *appear* to be. By appreciating and cooperating with the Divine Plan, and undergoing those changes that unfold the promise of God's Faith in His creatures, we experience not only the wonder, but also the eternal attributes of a life divinely-ordained and lived. We are invited beyond our present states of Knowingness, out of a Love that brings a nearness associated with an ever-increasing intensity, a brightness that runs through everything. This Beauty is all-encompassing, in a way never previously seen or experienced, bestowing upon us sensibilities and intelligent participation within all levels of the visible and invisible realms, to produce results that never cease to bring about wonder and amazement.

At a certain point in our development, we get a taste in the here-and-now of those ethereal worlds: out-of-body experiences bring that which is hidden to be observed; visions of nearness occur with those we love who are dimensionally far; the miracle of healing takes place; assistance comes inexplicably, when we need it the most. We are consciously aware of these events, and understand their Source.

Grateful and appreciative, we understand with absolute certainty our total dependency upon a Greater Power.

Death-and-return events offer a window into one or more worlds. *Dreams* that take years to unfold become the experiences now referred to in the past tense. *Out-of-body activities* take us to places and moments that give us a glimpse on the nature of this reality. Situations, resolved with help from the fifth- to the tenth-dimensions, further ignite an understanding found beyond the senses and the mind, communicated without words, so that we know when we need to know.

These encounters offer the individual entity opportunities to connect to, and understand, a whole much larger than the fraction one life represents. They allow the comprehension of life's immensity. *The importance of even one life* begins to unfold, when the limitations of this fractional and temporal, existential experience are lifted. When comparing these two aspects, the temporal and the eternal, the entity begins to know the entirety of life's meaning in terms of relationships, responsibilities, participations, contributions, and the joy derived from the progress a life well-lived brings.

When it is all said and done, each sentient, intelligent creature is a member of a social structure that is both diversified through the uniqueness of each individual, and unified through the fact that all of its creatures derive their existence from One Source. Moreover, this vast and diversified membership experience is a part of, on an ongoing basis, an omni-dimensional and multi-directional unified system of intelligent life. This Simulator contains creation *like an oven cooking everyone to perfection.* The system enables the conditions for all creatures to advance towards their Creator. Unable to control their individual destinies, or possess the results of each sojourn, the Soul-possessing and Spirit-connected Beings of Light are drawn inexorably towards their Maker.

With this kind of mileage, each entity endeavors, sooner or later to come to the realization of the One Truth of it All: we each are Beings able to become illumined, in transit and transcending from one to another worlds of God, within a built-in Program designed with a purpose. Just as an individual experiences an early termination of his or her fractional and temporal life, simply because of personal choices, or the choices of those around him, our civilization also is heading towards a similar outcome, because of our collective choices, within the theater of life on the planet. This termination may take longer, statistically speaking, yet sooner or later, as a species, we can erase ourselves from this earthly, existential experience.

We are supposed to learn from our history; from its inherent patterns there are messages that, time and again, signal the characteristics leading to self-destruction. We are so used to these cycles of annihilation, they seem to be eventualities we have all come to accept as inevitable.

Our individual and collective denials, signals unto themselves, remain unobserved and unaddressed. Why is this so?

When the Manifestations of God *appear* addressing this issue, They bring the solution which we are no longer able to recognize, despite the magnitude of the importance of the Truth for the cessation of our collective annihilation, and the associated suffering and pain over time. Disconnected from the Spirit and Soul, the majority of humanity rejects these Divine Physicians outright.

When we begin to listen to, and follow, Their Divine Message, centuries later, we witness a social transformation and the rise of a civilization bearing Their names, each and every time.

The motivating power fueling the rise of these civilization wanes over time simply because few, indeed, are the ones that listen and follow Their Divine Message.

Humanity fails, time and again, to experience the dictums that have come inscribed by the Pens of Glory within the Dream of a Creator whose Love and Compassion continues, despite our denial and refusal to listen to, and thus experience, the effects of those Messages. History repeats itself; we come and go in numbers, beyond the generations that form our recorded memories. Cycles upon cycles continue the never-ending loops that adorn those distracted from the Word and attached to material realms—those that are lost within themselves!

Chapter 10 - In the End

In this time period in human history, the main concern of each human entity should be—*how far or near am I to my Creator?*

Why is this important? Because the distance from the creature's heart—to the heart of the Creator—is the only thing that matters. Our virtues or vices, our choices to follow the road of the righteous or the road of the wicked, even such choices as whom to marry or what career to pursue, are all ultimately determined by the purity of our hearts as they are washed by the Ocean of God's Love.

Each life we experience runs on its own track of time. Some of these tracks of life overlap others, and for a while they run together, as a friendship, or a business deal. These events are meant to coalesce and bring about certain results that may, or may not, be expected. They represent opportunities the Simulator provides all travelers to build a sense of a reality all around us with a purpose, meaning, and a direction—objectives that may run concurrently towards a goal meant to bring enlightenment.

At other times, a rare event indeed, two tracks of life come together and coalesce eternally, resulting in the pairing of two independent lives into one eternal companionship.

Our lives are a theater of activities in which we participate and interact here and there, bringing about all sorts of effects, becoming parts of wholes, so that our lives unfold their own unique significances. Two or more of these life-tracks may merge, then suddenly draw apart, the participants never to encounter each other again. They may have finished a business deal, ended a war, or quarreled and walked away after being lovers. People move away from one another for so many reasons that we take for granted; yet, in the end, the tracks of all beings form the threads of the fabric of a reality written on the Scroll of Existence, held in time as records of a myriad lives, fractional and temporal, existential experiences, each a chapter that brings about a play, too many to know, with endless directions and objectives, many of which lead the actor into loops that repeat themselves over the canvas we think of as reality.

Each life, each thread of that fabric, runs in a track of time in infinity. At times, a single entity may be acting upon more than one track of time. He may be participating in parallel worlds in three or four activities that each move that entity towards different results, with objectives that may or may not end well, or may not end at all. How does he perform these omni-dimensional activities, affecting lives that interact for short or long periods of time, bonding temporarily, carrying the varying intentions of those participating, activities accruing into something else, a mix of thought-forms and feelings that carry all players in the game of life towards different and unique conclusions? How do we derive meaning from our lives within a grand Purpose that liberates, or imprisons each and all travelers during their fractional and temporal sojourns, their existential experiences?

We are not in control! We cannot hold onto anything of a third-or fourth-dimensional nature. These constructs come and go, props and practices we use to carry out our dreams within the Dream of a Creator, Whose numberless handlers help guide the many entities traveling through the oven of creation, cooking each and all to perfection.

Will the traveler find the way out? Or will he or she, instead, get lost within himself or her-self, forget the true Self, and be caught in the many loops that take each entity away from the Portal, that entry point that moves the traveler closer to the Beloved?

Divine Law

The theater of existence is wide open to myriad players pursuing their own games. What is that which you choose to do, each time, when you emerge from the Sea of Awareness onto the shores of consciousness—emerging from *Within into a world from Without*?

When understanding the Laws of God's Commandments, one must look deep into one's own heart for verification of the Truth. These Laws are never meant for one society only, or even for one world of nations. These Laws are meant for all Soul-possessing entities, of all places and times, Laws that refer to moral dictums meant to safeguard the unity of each planet.

There are other guidelines of a peripheral nature that fall under the umbrella of social mores and are applicable for a period of time, and are subjected to change, if, and when, society no longer requires them.

There was never a time when the Divine Laws did not exist. There was never a time when these Laws did not require the verification of, and the acting from the Spiritual hearts of all entities.

From Moses to the present, in this Adamic cycle, mankind, now in the age of spiritual maturity, has been made aware of these essential requirements to safeguard the unity of all, through a form of these Laws, known in the time of Moses as the *Ten Commandments*. Without universal agreement with this *Lesser Covenant* for all times, humanity would have remained in a state of ignorance much worse than it finds itself presently in.

What to do, then, when these binding Laws are broken by one's self, or by others. If it is one's self that has gone astray, we can ask God to forgive us and assist us, in changing our ways… the Simulator will bring the necessary experiences to bear upon the entity's understanding, charged with the necessary *special effects*, giving emphasis to the ramifications over time, and blending in the assistance of Handlers to ensure success for as long as the intention of the seeker's heart remains sincere.

If it is, on the other hand, another who has gone astray, we can pray to God to enlighten that individual. Never is it our right, or duty, to correct that individual, unless he or she poses a threat to himself, or to others.

We may, however, provide a gentle reminder by our own example, or by referencing sacred scripture, if the other Being wishes to listen. We need to understand that every entity undergoes, through his or her own sojourn of fractional and temporal, existential experiences, events related to his or her needs for development; that individual may need to make personal decisions that demonstrate a cause and effect within this, or future, time-frames.

When, therefore, a situation presents itself that is a moral test, it is best to take a *time out*, and to listen within one's own heart as to the correct action to take. This decision may take days, or weeks, or even months. Whatever the time it takes, it will be time well-spent.

Do not hurry. Do not worry. Let God lead the way, and all will be well.

We are dealing with a very sophisticated theater of interactive exchanges, meant to teach what all entities require to progress and become what God has designed for His creatures. Little by little, the effects of obedience, and the implementation of the Great and Lesser Covenants will, in fact, be witnessed by all.

Beneath the outward signs of obedience and its implementation, a flow of divine energetics comes with information, the waters-like blessings from within a unified system of intelligent life. Carrying what we need to improve and manage our third-dimensional requirements, these Blessings support our intention of advancing a divine civilization.

Over time, a civilization that behaves as one unit of life emerges, balanced and in harmony, coherent from within, and unified throughout the landscape of human endeavor. In this well-oiled living system, every member experiences the Love of God on a daily basis. This, and other planets of sentient and intelligent life, have yet to experience such Beauty, a Beauty which brings about *graduation*—and a move to Realms of unimaginable divine content. There is an urgency pressing on all entities everywhere: the need to search for the Beloved for this day and age of God. Discover and recognize this Manifestation of Perfection in order to jump-start one's life, to gain the necessary understanding that brings a clear focus, the certainty of walking in the right direction, and the knowing and fulfillment that can only come from the Source.

Chapter 11 - Outside the Simulator

Beyond the commentaries given by those who have gone through what we know of as near-death experiences, which pretty much are limited to the participants seeing a light tunnel, feeling immense love, and communicating with the figure of a Manifestation of God, and/or relatives, we don't seem to have enough knowledge to see beyond *the Simulator* that embraces us all during our sojourn established in a physiologically-based state of consciousness. One thing we can say is that these experiences, outside the parameters of a physiologically-centered state of consciousness, engender a different kind of observing and experiencing no longer based on the body-brain unit.

Since these events outside of brain-based consciousness were meant to occur in each and all cases, to the entities who experienced them, the relevant information was for each of them, and the benefit of those experiences was also meant to be unique to each one. Just like any other experience meant for each of us, these occurrences are events of direct benefit to each individual's stage of personal development, and bring the relevant information at the precise moment in the fractional and temporal, existential period for each seeker to understand something of extreme importance that assists in the propelling of that traveler from one to the next orbit of understanding, in order to move through one world to the next.

We have not heard of anyone besides the present author who has experienced ***near-death*** multiple times over a long period of time—over forty years. In fact, this author has experienced ***going to the other side*** more than half-a-dozen times, each occurrence different than the one before. By extracting the true meaning of these, and other, unique experiences, including out-of-body and healing events, he has opened up a new Realm of understanding that tells a more complete story of existence, a story of eternity that takes entities outside the Simulator— *the universal box* .

Included in the author's ***out-of-body*** experiences, of more than a dozen times, were those occurrences when he left his body interacting with others who, at the time, remained unaware that he had transferred the focus of his awareness elsewhere. At other times, when he was a speaker at a gathering, for example, he spoke to his audience about that which he was experiencing as his awareness travelled through the universe.

His ability to heal came about after his brief death in the dentist's chair. For a period of three years, he healed others, instantly and remotely, from various types of accidents as well as diseases. Most of those who were healed—or returned to life—were unaware of the cause of their new-found health.

All these distinctive experiences gave the author the omni-dimensional, and multi-directional, perspective enlightening this narrative.

By examining the results of all these experiences, as well as other phenomena, we may clarify the many points of view presented here in *the Simulator*, as well as in other books by the present authors: *Echoes of a Vision of... Paradise*, *if you cannot Remember*, *you will Return*, Volumes 1, 2, and 3, the *Synopsis*, and *Restoring the Heart*.

The authors have presented a narrative that opens a new perspective into what existence and the experiences of life represent for each of us, based on the cumulative effects of a life of exchanges and interactions with everything deemed relevant to all of us. This narrative offers a map that it is hoped may serve others in their individual journeys throughout unified systems of intelligent life, meant to help us develop the appropriate understanding and inner character that best reflects the intention and Dream of our Creator.

Using our first-hand experiences, as well as the unique experiences which others have shared with us, we have written these books explaining a more comprehensive Purpose for existence than the one presently held by many fellow travelers, a purpose of paramount importance for each entity to understand. This Dream, expressed multi-directionally in an omni-dimensional theater, offers many rich experiences meant to bring us nearer to our Beloved—as gradual states or conditions of purity of the heart.

Time is measured in milliseconds upon the Earth. Yet, in the higher realms, time is irrelevant.

Everything is happening all at once, according to God's decree. Plants spring up in less than an instant. Animals frolic in perfect meadows. Every heart is aligned to God's Will and Desire. From this Paradise, many planets like Earth are seen from a different perspective.

Lives are measured not in terms of time, but in terms of each one's heart-relationship to the Love of God. Since God's Love and Compassion are infinite, the progress of each entity is small indeed, as viewed within the compass of one mortal life.

And yet, God's Grace and Mercy are also infinite. So every tiny step each entity makes in fulfilling and serving the Will and Pleasure of his Creator is acknowledged—even celebrated—on High.

For this loving understanding of human frailty we can all truly be grateful.

In order to further understand the mechanics of the experience of existence, it is necessary to have the perspective of a Being who is outside creation—in a process of being developed towards a standard that graduates the entity.

Creation is the painting, and the Creator is the painter. In addition, for the entity known as human to have a proper orientation towards his or her temporal life-track, it is necessary to understand that track from within the purview of an endless, infinite framework in which neither *beginnings* nor *endings* are relevant concepts.

Suppose that you were to board a ship en-route in the middle of a great ocean, at a point where no shorelines could be seen. Then suppose, after traveling an indeterminate amount of time over numberless waves, you were to leave that ship and board another ship somewhere in the endless ocean.

Although you know that you have changed ships, still, as you look upon the waves, you cannot tell where you are in your journey.

This metaphor illustrates how most creatures continue helplessly upon their journeys of existence—with little knowledge of where they have come from, where they are, or where they are going.

In order to solve this conundrum of eternal existence, one must look up from the deck of the ship to discover, at dawn's tide, where the sun is rising.

That newly-risen Sun is the Manifestation, the Messenger of God, shining the new Light of Revelation which can allow ascension upon the power of His illumining Word, above the endless, circling ships of third- and fourth-dimensionally-based existences, into the heavens of Divine Love—a magnetic North to be guided therefrom.

No longer will your journey be without Purpose. That illuminating spark lit within Spirit and Soul now lights the way of God's Purpose for your own unique creation as a Soul-possessing, Spirit Being of

Light, headed for the polestar of your own divinely-created purpose in God's plan and Dream for you as the truly blessed and bowing servant.

All lives, past and present, become fused into this one, blissful condition of contentment. There is no longer anywhere to go because right where you are is the unity with His Love that you have always been looking for.

As the Love of God guides the ship of existence in this world, the Love of God opens the doors of the many worlds that follow. The Love of God assists in maintaining the right direction, through a deep feeling of joy, and the knowing with certainty that all is well.

There are many experiences along one's immeasurable sojourn confirming and assuring each traveler's direction, and furnishing the required information. When everything works well, as intended, the Simulator provides all the necessary special effects bringing the feed-back that makes sense of each step, enlightening the quester. The traveler sees enough ahead of a projected pattern to make the right choices for maintaining and/or correcting his direction as he responds to his own sense of Knowingness from within.

When you die, you are in fact *returning*, going back from within to your Self, the Light Being of Pure Awareness eternally existing at the tenth-dimension; just as, when you awaken in the morning, you come out of the box of the dream-world, a sojourn that embodies a fractional and temporal, existential experience. When you are born, you are in fact *returning* into the dream-world, of a mortal being back into the box, for another sojourn in a fractional and temporal, existential experience that holds opportunities for enlightenment, the realization of True Awakening. Thus we realize the mirroring effect, the reflection, taking place, again and again.

Our true-Self experiences the return, as our Soul-based state of awareness, tenth-dimensionally speaking, is withdrawn from the body we feel we occupy until our physiologically-based consciousness is turned off.

As the process of death reduces our mind-world construct and our physiologically-based state of consciousness, all the Spiritual, fifth-dimensionally-based mental attributes (thinking, comprehension, imagination, and memory), previously expressed fourth-dimensionally, slowly dim out the world we once partook of, and all that remains is our Soul-base awareness, as the material-construct vanishes without a trace.

In order to understand this process, of phase conjugation translating *one Reality into another reality*, assembling and later on disassembling, the moving forth, gating (birthing into) followed by a gating out (dying), in an omni-dimensional state *transferring our Soul-based awareness* into a space-time continuum, with multi-directional anticipated outcomes by a Simulator providing the required special effects that give all entities that sense of reality, an entity needs to remember the experience.

As immortal entities, we all exist outside of the Simulator, "*sleeping*" as Light Beings in the eternal Realm, a "***place***" referred to as a beginning that knows no beginning, simply because there is no entropic system to speak of, and time as we know it cannot be experienced. The properties of that singularity, and/or condition, are completely different; in fact, they are quite the opposite from the ones we find and experience on planet Earth. Knowing that which is eternal is how we can conceptualize, here, everything in terms of temporal time and spatial locations: because somewhere else, ***in that place***, we are all familiar with (but now cannot remember) the absence of time. In that eternity, spatial conditions are transparent, playing a different role, not one of separation requiring concepts of nearness and farness, but one of Oneness, where everything, anything in that Reality is always ever-present.

On one side of the mirror, here, within the Dream, the Simulator, we think and sense-perceive everything as being outside of each of us; when, in fact, everything experienced exists within us in our mind-world constructs, reflecting a world of names and appearances the way it does simply because the Simulator's properties anticipate and create everything that becomes manifested and considered as our reality, what we observe and understand, feel and come to experience.

On this side of the mirror, within the Simulator, the box, the construct of what is, is a temporal experience, no matter how large we measure that part of the created, in seconds, or hours, days, or years, or thousands or billions of years. The same applies to the space anything occupies; whether small or large, near or far, it is a temporal construct. All of these concepts are a part of, and the creation of, the Simulator. Outside of the Simulator, the opposite is true. Concepts of near or far, small or large, short or long, measured spatially, or based in units of time, do not exist. Nothing is far or near, and there is nothing measurable in terms of size or duration. The properties found on that side of the mirror are no longer reflections; they are Reality as created by God, in a Realm where eternity and perfection coexist and give rise to a unique system of life that knows no beginning or end.

Being there and being here give rise to our dual nature, the one expressing this material existence, and the other representing our divine source and true nature.

Each time we find our-Selves navigating the Sea of Awareness, within our Soul-based state of being, during a transfer, the process that takes each of us away from Reality into Un-reality (an Earth-type world), there are innate conditions that bring into effect the creation of a *bridge*, to interact and feel with, as soon as we reach the shores of consciousness with a unit or body. This physical unit is modulated locally (environmentally and genetically) within a unified system of intelligent life, also known as a fractional and temporal, existential experience, part and parcel of our heart's degree of separation—or nearness—from our True Selves.

We need a port-of-entry into these worlds of creation, to be initiated, conceived. There are infinite points of entry, each a point of return, too. We travel back and forth, a rinsing process for the entity's heart. We are in an eternal motion, heart-wise, and spatially-oriented. Our hearts address our relationship with our Creator; spatial separation relates to the needed condition appropriate for the entity's development—as a reward or punishment, advancing or moving away from the intended goal.

For as long as each of our hearts contains the impurities that prevent each of us from remaining in Reality—the way things should be—we instantly embark on journeys of return, again and again, back into and out of the Simulator, with the sole purpose of gradually purifying and becoming our True Selves, immortal Light Beings not required to incarnate in mortal worlds.

As the mirror-effect continues, we find ourselves in a loop reflecting our state of completeness, conditionally moved closer to, or further from, our Creator, Who measures each entity's development from the heart's state of purity, as patterns emerge in existence.

Our dual-nature serves one Purpose: His Dream of perfection encompassing our dreams, back and forth, coming to and awakening within the Dream of eternity, and then returning to find our-Selves within our dreams of mortal lives. The pattern tells, over time, the direction our decisions create, and our hearts signal the relevance of the journey, and how significant each moment experienced is—our states of Knowingness and Love stand witness to our Reality.

As entities, our sojourns continually offer opportunities to do the right thing, either as individuals, or collectively in groups, large or small. We are given the chance to act righteously in business, as students, as leaders of nations, and in so many other roles, too many to list here. Our decisions and the quality of our lives, whether we are just or unjust, bring our hearts closer to, or further from, God and our Selves. The less justly we act, the more the necessity for us to return and try again, until God releases us.

The further we move away from our true nature, our divine inheritance, the darker and more primitive worlds we will visit. These worlds offer pain and suffering the like of which we have never experienced. In the scheme of things, as an entity, you are not welcomed anywhere else. Reward and punishment are thus the pillars upon which our development rests. If we read and pay attention to the Holy Words inscribed in the Books revealed by the many Manifestations of God, we can clearly find messages referring to the conditions that await those that disobey, or act according to their vain and evil desires.

We are immortal entities whose existence cannot be extinguished. Howbeit, the quality and conditions of an environment shared and used to continue experiencing consciousness will attest to, and reflect, the traveler's gradual cleansing, or corruption, from one world to the next. Each heart is in constant communion and scrutiny by the Simulator, which anticipates and executes whatever is required to bring the proper realization to the traveler's state of understanding and love, in an attempt to awaken each entity and restore his direction towards God. A tug-of-war pulling each and all travelers ensues, time and again. The wicked, the oppressor, the evil doer, and the deceitful, all the ones ignoring the importance of existence, find themselves experiencing the effects of such lives. The effects of evil spill over, affecting others, generations away, with their virtual and material, negative consequences, growing until they become the fundamentals that bring down a civilization— until this influence changes for the better in an upward motion signaling advancement.

During each sojourn, an entity is given the required experiences that will gradually bring a greater understanding of a whole to be partaken of. Those special moments offer an insight into that other Reality, and what It means and offers, in contrast to an actuality (the way things are). We are always learning for as long as we are not distracted, or focused on things that are unimportant or unnecessary in our journeys. If we get caught up, attached and enslaved by any one thing, the pleasure that becomes an addiction of the flesh or the heart, for example, we begin to experience the patterns that bring about a loop.

When the heart of humanity was innocent and pure, the resultant understanding of life was *Truth Itself.*

In that state outside time, it was understood that God, the Creator, always was, and always would continue to be, All-Powerful. Because of this understanding, most of those entities known as human followed the straight path to God.

There were, however, those who believed that they could do better than their Creator, if given a chance; many still do. So, seeing into their hearts, God *gave them a chance* to prefer their own wills over His Will.

The results are the multiple types of worlds upon worlds that each of us sees today, and experiences inwardly (from with the Heart, or Soul, of the eternal Self existing in Perfection). These worlds of death and life, destruction and construction, happiness and suffering, created by the false and selfish desires of those who refused to surrender to the only One Who truly loved them. Thus were born the worlds of contrasts, names, and appearances.

When the entity returns from an experience as an incarnated being, potentially of Light (as a subject of enlightenment), and in transit, from a material world, he is moved as a sphere of pure awareness to his next phase of evolution. At this time, the unified system of intelligent life determines where he will *fit*. He may either incarnate again, as a mortal being, or leave the worlds of incarnation to move to the Realms of Light, or he may enter into a kind of suspended state to increase his illumination before he can be moved out of a projected, material-based loop in which his selfish desires may have trapped him.

Any being trapped in this kind of loop, between realms, requires extra assistance from beings of a higher Light frequency—often referred to as angels or handlers.

If the entity has obtained enough illumination to enter the light tunnel, that traveler will move through to an *exit* of the same light hue and intensity that he emits. The higher and brighter the intensity of Light, the more perfect, and closer to God's *Divine Plan*, is that corresponding world into which that Being will be placed, to continue the next step of the infinite spiritual journey upon which we are all embarked.

When the traveler enters this new, more perfect world, he has the chance to hone his own inner perfections or moral qualities, until eventually, over time, he becomes that which he was created to be—an entity exhibiting all the perfections in service to All-Mighty God. When that perfection is accomplished, according to the Will and Pleasure of the One Who sees deeply into each and every heart, that perfect entity may be chosen to play the role of an educator, a lesser prophet, and be in the station of the manifestation of his Lord.

Understanding the path to perfection allows us to honor the Manifestations of God. Theirs is a hard road, filled with grief and suffering, for They sacrifice all in the Service of Their Creator to uplift those Soul-possessing, Spirit beings who have forgotten their true purpose as humble and obedient servants of God.

Thus, the Manifestations sacrifice over and over, throughout infinite worlds and time-periods, to bring back entities, such as those known as human, from the abysm of perdition, selfish desires, and delusions, to the mountain top of praising God and His chosen Ones continuously, and without ceasing.

<u>Questioning the way things are to find Reality</u>.

Do you have a question? Pose it in the Simulator; the answers will come. Pay attention, and follow through on the experiences providing the answer. Wherever you are in your state of Knowingness, those questions are reflecting your present capacity as a traveler. The answers are in response to your call, those moment-to-moment offerings of enlightenment.

A pattern will develop over time, connecting all the dots of light of enlightenment, bringing a portal catapulting each entity into another womb for further development. These conditional-wombs hold each entity, for a while, in a nurturing environment meant to prepare the traveler, as a potential in transit and transcendence, for further worlds, opportunities that bring the traveler closer to the goal—reunion with the Beloved.

Experiences need to be analyzed, and questioned, as we ask ourselves, *how are they possible*? What does it take to bring them about? Avoid just experiencing life and moving on to the next moment. Each experience, from the point of view of the Simulator, is part of a complex set of routines, a program that involves a layering of structures, embedded and superposed into a unit, a system of intelligent life, which is a part of endless programs, all connected and executed as one process, carrying this universe, infinite in range and scope, one of many.

What is a *near-death* experience, for example? How is it possible to present and execute such an event to any entity in this plane of existence? What kind of an environment is realized to produce all the special effects that provide for such an experience, leaving no doubt in the awareness of the moving through dimensions, the gating out and back again, so that this flowing experience builds meaning, has a direction, and fulfills a purpose in line with a whole Knowingness meant to enlighten and bring closure to a question or questions preceding that event.

Dreams, which come in a variety of forms, present beautiful opportunities for us to discover their nature and assemble the experience of a non-linear domain—a past not followed by a future—where anything is possible, yet we sense-perceive without the physical instrumentation needed in this third-dimensional, material construct. They give the traveler the opportunity to investigate and explore, and eventually to figure out their nature and properties, their significance and dimensional place in the scheme of creation.

Visions offer an abundance of material to be analyzed. They may be offered in response to the myriad questions each being brings to the table. These events are bestowed to enhance our development, remind us to pay attention. Every event is designed for one particular entity. It is simply hearsay to another, just a nice story which is entertaining, at best, although others may have similar stories which, when shared, produce points of discovery.

Fifth-dimensional communications bring about an interconnectivity beyond the local unified system of intelligence, unveiling the universal mind in its localized form. This planetary unified system of intelligence allows for each species to have reciprocal activities beyond the range and scope of an individual's, or group's, consciousness.

The universal mind creates a lack of restrictions in terms of the obvious and not-so-obvious differing natures attributed to each species, including such factors as distance or time-frames, culture and language, and so many other diverse conditions that third- and fourth-dimensionally are considered as obstacles to communication. The fifth-dimensional, universal mind allows the transference of pertinent information between such diverse and different domains.

Healing, through the super-positioning of realities, is another example of the complex workings of the Simulator. These realities, dimensionally present as parallel constructs, are brought to bear on one another until they become integrated as one and the same time-track. Like formerly separate streams now flowing as one river, they link seamlessly in the continuum. This *superposing* brings health as an experience we think of as healing, integrated by stages, and having the effect of restoring the afflicted in order for the recipient to experience a condition known as "feeling healthy." The same process applies to the bringing about of sickness, as an effect of a condition we think of as direct or cross-contamination—resulting in disease.

Regardless of how critical and difficult to cure a sickness or condition of the body may seem to be, from the fourth-dimensional viewpoint, from the Knowingness of the fifth-dimension, that disease may be instantly reversed by an entity whose mission includes bringing about those effects. Healers' missions, whether utilizing medical science in their approaches, or more directly integrating medical science and spirituality, fifth-dimensionally, are to restore health as part of their calling of service to the whole. In each case, attitude and intention play the most crucial role as the dispensing of signals imposed upon the stand alone scalar carrier wave of the entity being treated, who is thus reprogrammed and assisted in the execution of the effect, the restoration of a healthy state.

This engineering of reality modifies outcomes in the general collective, through interactions either with a group, or an individual. A certain result is interfered with, or redirected as if it had never taken place, or, on a grand scale, made to take an alternate pathway to shift its outcome and impact on the consciousness of many. These conditional outcomes and their forerunning inputs become reseeded fifth-dimensionally, disassembling and restructuring conditions for a different outcome intent on buying more time, and/or demonstrate to the collective the right or wrong outcome under a controlled setting that covers ramifications beyond the need to inform and educate humanity.

Doctoring of reality, for example, regardless of how the effects are carried out and eventually manifested in restoring the collective health of a group or groups, follows a similar pattern of seeding the fifth-dimension. The necessary information is thus available to those whose roles are to bring about the delivery, as well as those that are the recipients, of that information, which will, over time, result in the appropriate changes; within the parameters and circumstances that emerge, all are educated to the subtle origin and transit of that which causes disharmony, the way it grows and brings about disease and suffering, and thus are able to avoid repeating the same behavior.

Since the Simulator can *anticipate* any and all inputs, and responds accordingly in a seamless way, there are entities whose *responses and sensibilities* allow for a mirroring of those anticipated outcomes as reflections within their own fourth-dimensional states of consciousness, their minds, allowing them to foresee, within certain limits of range and scope, those very same possible outcomes and predict the one most likely to occur. Again, this attribute, innately available to all entities, begs the question: *Are they helping to create a loop, or remove someone from one*? At this early stage of humanity's development, there is a need for caution. Since most of these entities, whose sensibilities allow them to foresee possible outcomes of certain conditions, have intentions and attitudes that are questionable at best, prudence would suggest waiting until such a world where these and many other abilities are commonplace in society, before trusting one's self to this type of information.

There is an unfortunate situation that unless such practitioners have evolved within their hearts to the required levels of purity and love, to assist those who consult in such matters, their advice will not bring positive results. Furthermore, those who ask for this kind of advice from others may be impaired or deterred from developing their own intuitive or fifth-dimensional abilities in listening for Higher guidance that can bring similar results, if and when needed—read your own book, ye traveler!

*

Transitioning from this plane to the next—"dying"—ordinarily should be as uncomplicated and as easy as going to sleep and awakening elsewhere. Complications arise when the body is not well, when the aging process brings to bear all sorts of anomalies resulting from contamination, and/or extreme wear of the organs, and terminal diseases that supplant an effortless transition (gated out) with an experience fraught with pain and suffering.

When an entity desires to advance through divine service in the worlds of God, he must accomplish three things. First and foremost, he must learn to surrender his will to that of His Creator's. Second, he must allow the necessary changes to be accomplished in his psyche—such as ridding himself of all attachments to the material world in which he presently resides, and instead attaching the very essence of his being to satisfying the Will and Pleasure of God.

Third, he must surrender to whatever outcome is pre-ordained for his transition from one realm of a lower nature or frequency to another realm of a higher, more spiritual and less material nature.

When, by God's design, this transition occurs, and the entity moves to a higher realm, that being of light knows without a doubt that his good fortune is totally due to the Grace and Mercy of God. For without God's Grace and Mercy, no entity has the purity or strength or the *reason* to move forward in nearness to His Compassionate Creator.

We would urge, therefore, all entities, known as human by agreement, to make it a first priority in their lives to surrender to God's Will and Pleasure, as indicated in part by His latest Manifestation. In so doing, they may gain the assurance necessary that the results of those actions which they have spent their lives accomplishing, during their fractional and temporal, existential experiences, have some value in the scheme of things.

Praise be to God, the All-Knowing, and the All-Wise.

As our love for God initiates the activities drawing us closer to His Love, and, in turn, healing and purifying the heart, our state of Knowingness—our Soul-based awareness—is, too, increasing.

Many indeed are the experiences that bring opportunities to adorn our true Selves with the attributes that reflect His Will and Pleasure during each sojourn. The traveler must learn to discriminate between what is right and what is wrong, to have correct intentions. He must be truthful above all things, to his true Self and to others, as he relies on God each moment of his existence. Indeed, in finding the Manifestation of God, the veils of unreality are rent asunder.

The more developed an entity becomes, the more consciously aware he is of a Reality previously hidden and considered far. A shift in his consciousness begins to occur, affecting his intentions and attitude, and the way he feels about life. There is an ever-increasing clarity and quality to the life experienced, a greater sense of belongingness, awe, and contentment; a feeling of gratitude and fulfillment adorns his inner Self.

The knowledge presented through these experiences liken to twenty-five letters, twelve hidden, and thirteen seen brought forth from the Mystery of Creation. Each of the hidden letters has a value expressed within the heart of the traveler.

For example, one letter residing within the innermost nature of the heart could be considered to represent the virtue commonly known as *compassion*. This inner quality allows the holder of that quality to be *akin to*, or *of kin with*, any and all creatures found within the universe.

Those who express this letter of the heart are able to transform the world surrounding them into a Paradise-like environment.

Another letter of the heart corresponds to what we think of as universal love. This quality of the heart allows the entity containing it to radiate the surrounding area with what is known as *pure joy*. Those expressing this letter illuminate their surroundings with the life-force of the Creator's *Heart*.

All the hidden and seen letters, taken together, form a composite of principles to live by for a holy life, blessed by God; that is, a life lived according to Moral Law, based in the divine order, rather than based on laws created by His creatures.

From this point of view, we can observe and understand the four kinds of love, the communication venues available that bring eternal life into play.

Our love for the Creator is first and foremost. In communicating our acknowledgement and appreciation, our detachment and our dependency on the Unknowable One, we confirm with certainty our state of true poverty and absolute nothingness.

God's Love for us is an ongoing renewal of His faith in each and all of His creatures, assuring and blessing, guiding and never abandoning us, through His Grace. The Eternal Realm is for-ever inviting us to experience the significance of both the Divine Plan and Reunion with Him.

The Love of God for Himself is the Source and the First Cause of All That Is, without a beginning or an end. The Creator Knows of His Love, and this Love flows eternally with the blessings that each and all of His creatures need.

The Love we all share is a communication of trust and an expression of the bond that exists among His creatures. It is the means to any end that is good. This Love of God promotes all relationships without exception, assuring the advance of civilization—when each member of society is integrated, and connected deep within, to God.

The Love of God is the Life that flows eternally, like the blood that flows within our veins. It is the carrier of existence that emerges as our Soul-centered, Self-awareness, and much more.

Love rises from its Mysterious Foundation with no beginning, bringing together what needs to be coupled and coalesced. It rises in purpose and charges the recipients with added functionality, growth, and instinctive intelligence in the mineral, plant, and animal kingdoms until finally, in humankind, it becomes human love. When the Soul-possessing Spirit being of Light directs this love back to the Creator, the entity then consciously receives His Love, *is transformed*, and transcends a third- and fourth-dimensional state of consciousness. The human state is brought into a higher domain, the entity becoming consciously aware of his higher-Self. No longer forgetful and lost, the creature bonds with the Creator, and advances to the summit of Reunion with the Beloved.

This indescribable encounter is transformative and profound—unique to each immortal being. The eternal becomes accessible and ever-present, the world is now changed, and Paradise unveils Its wings so that the eternal servant may experience the Realms of glory.

In contrast, entities who are stuck in a muddle in the fandango of pride, greed, jealousy, envy, anger, and hatred are consumed and enmeshed in the lowest possible state of consciousness. Their behavior is pathetic at best; at worst, it is objectionable to obscene and abhorrent, in contrast to the behavior that uplifts and sustains—an eternal and joyful ride.

Chapter 12 - The Point of it All

In between this world and the next is a substance known as *the etheric field or vacuum,* (in reality a plenum) that exists throughout the universe to separate the worlds, or realms of existence. When a creature crosses the threshold between this world and the next-destined realm, that creature gets transformed instantly from the materialized being that it was, to a sphere of pure awareness, *a focused point* expressing its state of development, and centered in the etheric field separating the worlds.

In that state or condition that holds its state of awareness, the creature is aware of existing as a point of pure awareness, bereft of attachments to anything other than its Creator, the God of all.

When in this state, the lonely creature becomes humbled by the infinitude that surrounds it, while being immersed in a *Sea of Awareness*, within and without, as a reminder of the singleness of its nature.

When in this state, the creature realizes that all the material success—or failure—that it may have achieved in the last sojourn is worth nothing. It is aware of its true worth, an ever-present nothingness in the presence of Almighty God.

This realization brings either contentment in a state of infinite servitude, or regret and continuous fear of separation and solitude.

We are each this point of entry or exit at all times. There is never a moment when the very awareness which each of us is, is not it-Self dependent upon the Will and Pleasure of the All-Mighty. There is not a moment when each of us is not dependent upon the All-Bountiful One for his very existence.

This utter poverty of Self and utter richness of God is an evident fact of existence that cannot—and should not—ever be denied. To deny it is to determine one's road traveling in the opposite direction of nearness to God. To deny God's All-ness is to seal one's *death* of the Spirit. It is only God's Wealth of Grace and Mercy that ever allows us to live the life of His faithful servants—and thus be filled with the true life, the flame of His Love that burns ever and forever.

This is the Grace and Mercy of God… without that Grace each of us is less than dust. An entity in that state of separation and remoteness cannot be observed in the etheric field, lacks the eternal light of life in God through His ever-present Love, and is bound to the returns and descent of mortal worlds in order to up-bring the intensity of his awareness of God, again and again.

The Light of God, His Love, shines within each of us, at the core of who we are. It is the engine of each creature; that Love cannot be ignored, or Its existence denied. It is essential to existence, and the foundation of all there is. To refute the presence of His Love, or act in ways contrary to the Nature of this Love, is to condemn one's Self to the remoteness and isolation of a state of near-absolute deprivation.

When we peruse the skies at night with the light of a full moon, we can attest to an immensity that leaves us all in awe. Imagine then, worlds upon worlds, each infinite in range and scope, and each of us as travelers, exploring and discovering our true objectives, including the significance of our creation. How do we find our way in that immensity?

Each and every Manifestation of God, the Creator, gives each of us the opportunity to be absorbed in His Love, comingled and coalesced again and again, to feel fulfilled with His Love, nurtured and guided once more through the Sea of Awareness, thankful in pleasing the Creator's Will and Pleasure, *travelers towards the Light that never fades.*

As our individual dreams fade and give way to the only True Dream and Dreamer, we come to a Reality that was meant to be our true home. So many experiences have come and gone. Throughout lifetimes, so many changes have taken place, so many chances taken in the name of love, a love that appeared and vanished, time and again.

Beyond and through the veils of our imagination, we find concealed the Key that opens all the doors, portals of entry that give and bring the substance of a Reality that is always present, an eternal, ever-consuming desire for the Love of God.

We leave the traveler with this note: *Never cease to search* for the Truth, the Way, and the Light that can only be found in, and through, His Manifestations. They are, truly, the only way to His Love.

Entities, human by agreement, potentials in transit and transcendence, Soul-possessing, Spirit Beings, gated in and out, piped through tunnels of Light, modulated from within and from without, respond to the many opportunities to serve one another, or not, to advance in Knowingness and Love—become enlightened—or not. Each fractional and temporal, existential experience is a rare opportunity to discover He Whom God Manifests, a golden chance offering the means to heal and coalesce the Soul-based state of awareness with the Spirit Being, mind, and body, and thus to Remember and Return.

We leave the reader with this important note: Because of the various properties of Creation specific to the Simulator, its embedded, layered, and superposed nature, the spatial properties affecting the relationship of the various omni-dimensional states are measured neither in terms of space, nor in time. There is no distance to be traveled or time to elapse, when transitioning from the outside and into the Simulator, or from within to outside, as both are the effects of the gradual purification of the traveler's heart and his state of Knowingness. The transfer occurs independent of the third-dimensional characteristics we identify with the concepts of time and space.

These conditional states of separation are heart- and Knowingness- based, as expressions of the degree of purity and clarity found there. We move closer, to or farther from, God. This simply means that we are accepted into worlds that are far more perfect and beautiful, or not, yet they all reside within the same One Point of Light.

Books by Kito and Ling Productions

www.loginthesoul.com

For Adults:

Echoes of a Vision of Paradise:

If You Cannot Remember, You Will Return, Volumes 1 – 3

Echoes of a Vision of Paradise:

If You Cannot Remember You Will Return, a Synopsis

Restoring the Heart

The Simulator:

a dream within a Dream

For Children:

www.loginthesoul.org

Andy Ant and Beatrice Bee

Beauty is on the Inside

Bee and Fairy Power:

(A short of novel in which the Beings of Nature use the super-power Virtue of Love to help humans Grow Organically)

How Alexander the Gnome Found the Sun

Katie Caterpillar Finds Her Song

Return to Paradise:

(a short novel in which Happy the Blue Bird, and Bright-Wings the Cardinal use Virtues to bring back Paradise)

The King and the Castle:

Love Flies in on the Wings of Destiny

Acknowledgment

The authors want to mention with gratitude that the adult series listed under *Books by Kito and Ling Productions* were a Spiritual, fifth-dimensional cooperation with the many entities meant to assist human development, as well as the Manifestations of God Whose Writings influenced the general viewpoint painting this landscape.

Kito and Ling Production-Copyright 2015

About the Author

Frank Scott and Nisa Montie joined forces to aid the enlightenment of humanity. Since his youth, Frank has been gifted with unusual experiences that inform and give a map that helps direct each entity on the divine path of Truth. Nisa uses animal and fairy characters to teach virtues in joy-filled children's tales.